Acknowledgments

It is with deep gratitude that we acknowledge the many educators who so generously contributed their expertise to this work. We would especially like to thank:

Jennifer Anderson, Island Trees Union Free School District, New York

Suzy Caceres, Hicksville Union Free School District, New York

Sarah Cioffi, Shenendehowa Central School District, New York

Marialice B.F.X. Curran, PhD, Founder, The Digital Citizenship Institute, Connecticut

Katie DiGregorio, PhD, West Hempstead Union Free School District, New York

Omar Garcia, Hicksville Union Free School District, New York

Mariel Gómez de la Torre-Cerfontaine, Rowan-Salisbury Schools, North Carolina

James Housworth, Roseville Area High School, Minnesota

Helaine W. Marshall, PhD, Long Island University Hudson, New York

Judy Goris-Moroff, Huntington Union Free School District, New York

Christina Moser, North Merrick Union Free School District, New York

Maria Zambuto, Oyster Bay-East Norwich School District, New York

Our most heartfelt appreciation goes out to our editor, Dan Alpert, for believing in our work and for graciously offering his guidance and support throughout the project. Our sincere appreciation also goes to the entire Corwin team, especially to Lucas Schleicher and Mia Rodriguez, for their diligent and attentive work on the manuscript preparation and production process.

TABLE 8.2 ● Technology Readiness Survey

1. Which digital learning resources do you use? Why? In what way do these tools provide instructional support for English Learners?
2. What challenges do you face in designing and managing your digital-age learning ecosystem?
3. What support do you need to effectively integrate digital learning resources into your classroom?
4. How does your physical and virtual classroom support interactive group work?
5. Does the physical and virtual learning space allow you to interact freely with groups?
6. How confident are you when using technology in remote, in-person, and hybrid learning environments?
7. What are the key skills your students will develop while working within your digital-age learning ecosystem?

ADOPT, DON'T SHOP! GRADES 2-4

In this project students learn about animal cruelty and record videos of themselves reading to pets to promote fluency and command of the English language. Students engage and educate community members about the benefits of adopting a pet and the different ways that animals can help people build confidence, increase relaxation, and reduce anxiety.

(This lesson seed was adapted from a lesson created by Jennifer Anderson, Michael F. Stokes Elementary School, and Christina Moser, Old Mill Road School.)

STUDENT GOALS

- I can write a friendly letter
- I can compare and contrast an animal shelter and a pet store
- I can educate others about animal homelessness, pet care, and pet adoption

ACTIVATE
Students participate in an interactive Nearpod presentation that highlights important information about dog and cat homelessness, overpopulation, and the differences between animal shelters, pet stores, and puppy mills.

CREATE
Students poll their classmates, family members, and friends to find out if they own a pet and how they got their pet. (For example, pet store or adoption center, or other.)

Digital-Age Teaching for English Learners

Second Edition

To my husband Eric, for his eternal love and devotion -
and to Holly, Noah, Liam, and Emily, our shared joy. – HR

Thank you for the love, joy, and laughter you have brought to my life -
Eladio, Justin, Jared, Jillian, and Papa. – LE

I dedicate this book to my family, who are my daily inspiration -
Howie, Benjamin, Jacob, and Noah. – AH

Digital-Age Teaching for English Learners

A Guide to Equitable Learning for All Students

Second Edition

Heather Rubin

Lisa Estrada

Andrea Honigsfeld

A SAGE Publishing Company

FOR INFORMATION:

Corwin

A SAGE Company

2455 Teller Road

Thousand Oaks, California 91320

(800) 233-9936

www.corwin.com

SAGE Publications Ltd.

1 Oliver's Yard

55 City Road

London, EC1Y 1SP

United Kingdom

SAGE Publications India Pvt. Ltd.

B 1/I 1 Mohan Cooperative Industrial Area

Mathura Road, New Delhi 110 044

India

SAGE Publications Asia-Pacific Pte. Ltd.

18 Cross Street #10-10/11/12

China Square Central

Singapore 048423

President: Mike Soules

Associate Vice President and Editorial
   Director: Monica Eckman

Program Director and Publisher: Dan Alpert

Senior Content Development Editor:
   Lucas Schleicher

Associate Content Development
   Editor: Mia Rodriguez

Editorial Assistant: Natalie Delpino

Production Editor: Megha Negi

Copy Editor: Integra

Typesetter: Hurix Digital

Cover Designer: Candice Harman

Marketing Manager: Sharon Pendergast

ISBN: 978-1-0718-2446-7

This book is printed on acid-free paper.

21 22 23 24 25 10 9 8 7 6 5 4 3 2 1

Contents

Visit the companion website for *DATELs* resources
and related materials at
resources.corwin.com/DigitalAgeTeachingforELs

Acknowledgments

It is with deep gratitude that we acknowledge the many educators who so generously contributed their expertise to this work. We would especially like to thank:

Jennifer Andersen, Island Trees Union Free School District, New York

Suzy Caceres, Hicksville Union Free School District, New York

Sarah Cioffi, Shenendehowa Central School District, New York

Marialice B.F.X. Curran, PhD, Founder, The Digital Citizenship Institute, Connecticut

Katie DiGregorio, PhD, West Hempstead Union Free School District, New York

Omar Garcia, Hicksville Union Free School District, New York

Mariel Gómez de la Torre-Cerfontaine, Rowan-Salisbury Schools, North Carolina

James Housworth, Roseville Area High School, Minnesota

Helaine W. Marshall, PhD, Long Island University Hudson, New York

Judy Goris-Moroff, Huntington Union Free School District, New York

Christian Moser, North Merrick Union Free School District, New York

Maria Zambuto, Oyster Bay-East Norwich School District, New York

Our most heartfelt appreciation goes out to our editor, Dan Alpert, for believing in our work and for graciously offering his guidance and support throughout the project. Our sincere appreciation also goes to the entire Corwin team, especially to Lucas Schleicher and Mia Rodriguez, for their diligent and attentive work on the manuscript preparation and production process.

Publisher's Acknowledgments

Corwin gratefully acknowledges the contributions of the following reviewers:

Shaeley Santiago
English Learner Coordinator
Ames Community School District
Ames, Iowa

Shawnna Sweet
Professional Development Specialist
Mid-West Regional Bilingual Education Resource
Network (RBERN)
Rochester, New York

Isabel Tuliao
Literacy Program Coordinator
Klein ISD
Spring, Texas

About the Authors

Heather Rubin is the Administrative Coordinator for the New York State Education Department's Long Island Regional Bilingual Education Resource Network (LIRBERN) at Eastern Suffolk BOCES. She presents regularly at national and international conferences on topics related to instructional design and technology integration for English Learners and provides school districts with professional learning and guidance in order to support the needs of English Learners and their families. She has over 20 years of experience as a teacher, administrator, and education consultant. Her career as an ESOL professional began as a high school teacher for the NYC Board of Education and for Roosevelt UFSD in Long Island, NY. She has worked as an adjunct professor for Queens College, Molloy College Graduate School of Education, Hofstra University, and at Mercy College. Her combined expertise on ELs and the use of technology to support learning developed while working for the Board of Cooperative Educational Services of Nassau County (Nassau BOCES) where she was first an ESOL Program Specialist for the NYSED Bilingual/ESL Technical Assistance Center and then the Program Coordinator of Model Schools/Digital Age Teaching and Education. She holds a master of science in education degree for teaching English to speakers of other languages from Queens College, City University of New York, and a professional diploma in school district leadership from Fordham University. She co-authored *ELL Frontiers Using Technology to Enhance Instruction for English Learners* (2017), with Lisa Estrada and Dr. Andrea Honigsfeld, published by Corwin. She is also the co-contributor of *Digital Age Teaching for English Learners* in The Handbook of TESOL in K-12 (2019), a Wiley publication.

Lisa Estrada is recently retired from her position as the Supervisor of English as a New Language, Bilingual Education, and World Language Programs at Hicksville Public Schools, Hicksville, New York. She was also an adjunct professor in the Molloy College Clinically-Rich Intensive Teacher Institute, Rockville Centre, New York.

Her educational experience and training includes over 30 years of ESL and Bilingual Education in K–12 settings. She was the recipient of the 2020 Outstanding Long Island ESOL Administrator of the Year Award presented by the Long Island Professional Committee on ESOL Education. She co-authored *ELL Frontiers Using Technology to Enhance Instruction for English Learners* (2017), with Heather Parris and Dr. Andrea Honigsfeld, published by Corwin. She is also the co-contributor of *Digital Age Teaching for English Learners* in The Handbook of TESOL in K-12 (2019), a Wiley publication.

Through her extensive knowledge of the education of ELs, she provides technical assistance and professional development on effective differentiated strategies, culturally responsive teaching, and technology integration for administrators and teachers working with English Learners. She conducts workshops and presents regularly at regional, national, and international conferences.

Andrea Honigsfeld, EdD, is Associate Dean and Professor in the School of Education and Human Services at Molloy College, Rockville Centre, New York. She directs a doctoral program in Educational Leadership for Diverse Learning Communities. Before entering the field of teacher education, she was an English-as-a-foreign-language teacher in Hungary (Grades 5–8 and adult) and an English-as-a-second-language teacher in New York City (Grades K–3 and adult). She also taught Hungarian at New York University.

She was the recipient of a doctoral fellowship at St. John's University, New York, where she conducted research on individualized instruction. She received a Fulbright Award to lecture in Iceland in the fall of 2002. In the past 18 years, she has been presenting at conferences across the United States, Canada, China, Denmark, Great Britain, the Philippines, Sweden, Thailand, and the United Arab Emirates. She frequently offers staff development, primarily focusing on effective differentiated strategies and collaborative practices for English-as-a-second-language and general-education teachers. She coauthored *Differentiated Instruction for At-Risk Students* (2009) and co-edited the five-volume *Breaking the Mold of Education* series (2010–2013), published by Rowman and Littlefield. She is also the co-author of *Core Instructional Routines: Go-To Structures for Effective Literacy Teaching, K–5 and 6–12* (2014) and author of *Growing Language and Literacy* (2019) published by Heinemann. With Maria Dove, she co-edited *Coteaching and Other Collaborative Practices in the EFL/ESL Classroom: Rationale, Research, Reflections, and Recommendations* (2012) and *Co-Teaching for English Learners: Evidence-based Practices and Research-Informed Outcomes* (2020). Maria and Andrea also co-authored *Collaboration and Co-Teaching: Strategies for English Learners* (2010), *Common Core for the Not-So-Common Learner, Grades K–5: English Language Arts Strategies* (2013), *Common Core for the Not-So-Common Learner, Grades 6–12: English Language Arts Strategies* (2013), *Beyond Core Expectations: A Schoolwide Framework for Serving the Not-So-Common Learner* (2014), *Collaboration and Co-Teaching: A Leader's Guide* (2015), *Coteaching for English Learners: A Guide to Collaborative Planning, Instruction, Assessment, and Reflection* (2018), and *Collaborating for English Learners: A Foundational Guide to Integrated Practices* (2019), seven of which are Corwin bestsellers. She is a contributing author of *Breaking Down the Wall: Essential Shifts for English Learner Success* (2020).

Preface

So much has changed since our first edition of this book was published in 2017. In *ELL Frontiers: Using Technology to Enhance Instruction for English Learners*, we were just beginning our collective journey toward creating classrooms infused with technology tools. This second edition, now entitled *Digital-Age Teaching for English Learners*, arrives at a consequential and momentous time in the history of education.

As the world still reckons with the impact of the COVID-19 pandemic, we acknowledge that teachers are working with more creativity, commitment, and persistence than ever before to provide students with meaningful learning experiences. The dramatic transition to remote and hybrid learning models has made it essential for all teachers to develop, nurture, and expand their pedagogical skills for the digital age in order to fully embrace what technology may offer and to maintain our connection with students and their families academically, linguistically, socially and emotionally in a virtual world.

This book also arrives at a time of unapologetic calls to eliminate all forms of bias and inequity in our classrooms and larger communities alike. Let us commit to providing all students with *historically, culturally,* and *linguistically* responsive and sustaining educational practices that value students' rich cultural, linguistic, and racial identities as well as offer much needed support for their social-emotional growth and development.

We have expanded our chapters to address these essential topics and provide research-informed and evidence-based practical teaching strategies that can be used every day. We hope this book will support all teachers to meet this moment with new resolve to promote equitable access to engaging and enriching digital-age educational opportunities for our English learners.

THE DIGITAL DIVIDE

A recent study noted that "Even in states with the smallest digital divides one in four students still lack adequate internet" (Chandra et al., 2021, p. 3). Schools around the world are striving to close the digital divide and bridge the opportunity gap for historically marginalized students. This is particularly true for many English learners (ELs). Access to devices, or experience with technology or the Internet, may present challenges to newly arrived families. For ELs, remote and hybrid learning may present challenges such as using unfamiliar digital learning resources and securing ongoing support to troubleshoot technical difficulties in a new language they are just developing. Today more than ever, there is a great sense of urgency to understand and respond to the complexities in providing equity and accessibility for ELs.

ENGLISH LEARNERS OF THE FUTURE

In this new and evolving learning environment, traditional practices such as explicit teaching of grammatical structures and direct instruction in the four domains of listening, speaking, reading, and writing in order to achieve communicative competence in English are no longer sufficient. The digital-age English learner must become adept at the six language domains of listening, speaking, reading, writing, viewing, and visually representing. In addition, we must commit to providing ELs with rigorous instruction that addresses the 5 Cs (critical thinking, communication, collaboration, creativity, and culture), as well as complex, grade-level academic content. This is no small feat! In this book we invite you to work together to find innovative ways to foster digital literacy and provide English learners with targeted, student-centered instruction that also clears the pathway to authentic language, literacy, and technology practices. By modeling the appropriate use of technology and engaging English learners with the tools and strategies in this book, our hope is that you will not only improve academic outcomes and enhance language and literacy development but also cultivate digital citizenship in an equitable, joyful, authentic learning environment.

A word about terminology: Across the United States and internationally, students coming to school from homes where languages other than English are spoken are referred to in a number of ways. In this book, we will refer to the students as English learners (ELs) and the instructional approach as English Language Development/English as a Second Language (ELD/ESL). We recognize that a substantial part of the EL population participates in bilingual education and many students speak two or more languages. This book addresses the needs of these bilingual and multilingual students and their teachers as well.

We also recognize that many new terms have emerged to describe various instructional technology integration models and practices. We identify and describe this terminology and provide examples throughout the book. You will find clear explanations of each of the following: virtual learning; remote, hybrid, and in-person learning; asynchronous vs. synchronous learning; and flipped learning. We will explain how they fit into to your own digital-age learning ecosystem and how these instructional delivery methods benefit English learners.

OVERVIEW OF CHAPTERS

What is necessary to implement effective digital-age instruction for English learners (ELs)? Each chapter of the book addresses different essential elements to answer this question. We include timely, thought-provoking, and tangible ways for teachers to create their own digital-age learning ecosystem that is engaging, equitable, and allows students to have voice and choice in their learning journey. While each chapter takes a unique angle, there will be several recurring features:

 ### DIGITAL-AGE LEARNING EXPERIENCE

This section provides an overview of current technology integration models and instructional strategies along with application of those resources to ELD/ESL instruction. Under the heading *Remote and Hybrid Learning Environments* we highlight information specific to designing and delivering instruction within in-person, remote, and hybrid learning environments.

 ### UNDERSTANDING ELs

The *Understanding ELs* section in each chapter offers specially selected methodologies and recommended strategies directly connected to the theme of the chapter. These research-informed strategies in support of ELs' language and literacy development were chosen based on seminal publications and current research studies.

 ### MAKE-IT-YOUR-OWN LESSON SEEDS

With a unique focus on ELs' academic and linguistic needs, we have included sample lesson seeds as examples that can be adapted for use in any classroom. Each lesson seed includes learning targets, as well as strategies for activating students' prior knowledge and promoting engagement and collaboration. The lesson seeds are intended to demonstrate how ELs can be supported with scaffolded instructional strategies infused with digital learning resources. The lesson seeds serve as a quick reference of ideas to help you in the deeper development of a comprehensive lesson plan. You can add your own strategies and content when expanding the lesson seed and may even adapt the template for use as a HyperDoc for students.

 CONSIDER THIS

In each chapter we invite you to consider the topic from multiple perspectives. Under the heading *Opportunities for Collaboration*, we make recommendations on how to foster collaborative practices with colleagues. We will discuss ways that ELs' *Social-Emotional Needs* may be addressed to support *Building Resilience* as well as highlight *Culturally Responsive-Sustaining Educational Practices*. Finally, we invite you to extend the information in the chapter beyond the classroom. In the subsection entitled *Resources Outside the School Context,* we consider how key ideas, tools, and recommendations are transferable or applicable to students' lives outside the school context.

 DIGITAL-AGE EXPLORER'S CORNER

In order to provide a vision for the digital-age classroom, we share vignettes from educators who are bravely exploring the digital-age classroom by incorporating technology into their in-person, remote, and hybrid learning environments in creative ways.

 PLN QUESTIONS

To facilitate discussions about ELD/ESL methodology and the development of your own digital-age learning ecosystem, you will find targeted questions at the end of each chapter that encourage conversations based on the central themes and ideas presented. We encourage you to create professional learning networks (PLNs) within your own immediate school or district context or within online communities. To ensure a comprehensive approach, try to build your PLN so it is composed of content area, ELD/ESL, and technology specialists and make every effort to extend participation in the virtual space via social networks, blogs, and media outlets such as Twitter, Facebook, Instagram, and YouTube. #ELLchat and #MLLChat_BkClub are two examples of very popular PLNs that engage educators from all around the world.

 TOOLS AND RESOURCES

We offer supplementary tools and resources at the end of the book. A complete list of technology resources is provided in

Appendix A. ELD/ESL methodology resources are provided in Appendix B.

These are exciting times for technology integration! As a result of the pandemic, and the continual evolution of technology, all students—English learners, multilingual learners, and their English-proficient peers—have experienced significant changes in their personal and academic lives. Technology is now at the core of our daily routines, teaching and learning processes, and social interactions as well. Let us continue to harness the benefits of it for our students' language, literacy, and social-emotional growth!

CHAPTER 1

Digital-Age Teaching for English Learners

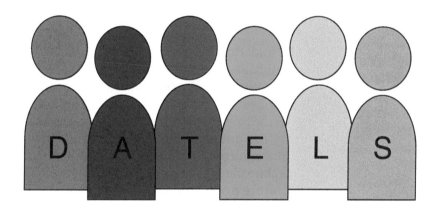

If we teach today as we taught yesterday, we rob our children of tomorrow.

(Dewey, 1944, p. 167)

MULTILITERACIES, MULTIMODALITIES, AND LEARNING ECOLOGIES

We all remember the spring of 2020. A pandemic hit the world and suddenly, everything changed. Just about everything seemed to have shut down overnight, and learning went remote. Administrators and teachers worked together to devise strategic plans to deliver instruction in a way that, for many educators, was entirely new. Many agree that the pandemic was a catalyst for change in the education world. Now, it is no longer about how we use technology to provide access to daily lessons or to enhance content and language instruction for English learners. Our focus has shifted from how to use technology to support English learners, to how to use technology to create digital-age learning ecosystems for ELs. The emphasis on the development of multiliteracies for ELs through the use of digital learning resources is a necessary shift in TESOL methodology. The development of receptive and expressive language skills in the digital age includes not only listening, speaking, reading, and writing but also viewing and visually representing. This book is an introduction to creating digital-age learning environments that support English Learners. Digital-Age Teaching for English Learners (DATELs) is a student-centered, technology-infused approach that increases opportunities for contextually rich, authentic language practice while promoting 21st-century literacy skills. A DATELs approach engages students in synchronous and asynchronous learning opportunities that provide flexible access to deeper academic content, while also developing language skills.

We have also come to understand that the digital age requires the development of multiliteracies and the use of multimodalities for language acquisition and effective communication beyond the classroom (Lesaux, 2016; Vance, 2006). The term *multiliteracies* is of specific relevance to language learners as it encompasses not only the understanding of the various new ways in which we communicate because of advancements of technology, but also acknowledges linguistic diversity and the intersectionality of culture and language. The framework for traditional forms of communication in any given language is bound to a dominant culture (New London Group, 1996; Sang, 2017). Understanding and developing multiliteracy skills provides ELs with equitable access to content and culturally responsive means of expression. This means that we explicitly teach all six literacy skills (listening, speaking, reading, writing, viewing, and visually representing), as students use multiple modalities to engage in the 5 Cs of 21st-century learning: communication, collaboration, creativity, critical thinking, and culture. In this book we'll examine current understandings of digital-age education and explore how we can improve instructional methodology for English learners to meet the complex demands of this new era.

THE DIGITAL-AGE LEARNING EXPERIENCE

THE CLASSROOM SETTING

There are many new terms to define the classroom setting in the digital age. Unlike traditional classrooms which existed only in a physical space, today's classroom includes both a physical space and a virtual space. Both the physical and the virtual learning environment allows for synchronous and asynchronous classroom experiences. Synchronous instruction occurs at the same time but does not necessarily take place within the same space (e.g., instruction delivered using live video conferencing tools such as Zoom or Google Meet or delivering instruction to students in person in a physical classroom). Asynchronous instruction occurs not only in different spaces but also at different times (e.g., self-paced online classes, pre-recorded video tutorials, independent study). Protocols for designing and implementing synchronous and asynchronous learning experiences are required for students to work successfully whether they are in-person, remote-only, or in a hybrid setting. Whether we deliver instruction entirely in-person, remotely, or in a hybrid combination of the two, designing learning ecologies to advance language development and content knowledge require that we consider the way we want students to interact with one another, learn by doing, and express their ideas using digital learning resources (WIDA, 2014).

This book explores how we can we leverage these classroom environments to increase interaction and engagement to better serve our English learners.

THE 5 Cs FOR 21st-CENTURY LEARNING

Student interaction is directly aligned with the goals established in the Partnership for 21st-century learning framework (2019). The P21 Framework pioneered the identification of four 21st-century skills most important for K–12 learners. These skills became known as the 4 Cs—critical thinking, communication, collaboration, and creativity. However, we have added a fifth "C"— Culture—to include culturally responsive and sustaining practices that recognize and affirm the diversity that all learners bring to the classroom.

The 5 Cs should be integrated into daily instructional practices for ELs:

Critical thinking. Linking learning across subjects and disciplines and assisting ELs in developing background knowledge. Using technology to reduce or remove language barriers so that ELs can decipher problems and find solutions.

Communication. Providing numerous opportunities for ELs to share thoughts, ask questions, and discuss ideas and solutions with their peers. This could include the use of translation apps, podcasts, blogs, video chats, social media, and online discussion boards.

Collaboration. Creating projects that allow ELs to work with classmates both in class and virtually to achieve a shared goal, while contributing their own talent and expertise. This requires the use of tiered tasks and scaffolded assignments that are accessible in an online learning management system.

Creativity. Helping ELs express their thoughts, ideas, and content knowledge creatively. This can be achieved through the use of multimedia resources and project-based learning activities that help ELs use the target language to make real-life connections to learning.

Culture. Recognizing that ELs bring rich cultural and linguistic experiences to the classroom and building on them whether working in person or virtually in remote learning environments. It is essential that ELs make meaningful connections between the home and school cultures and develop their unique cultural identities. Design collaborative projects that demonstrate an acceptance and appreciation for cultural diversity. This involves including the global community and respecting the needs of those who are collaborating from different cultures, building an awareness for all students of how culture impacts an individual's or group's choices, and providing a forum for discussions related to multiculturalism.

DIGITAL-AGE TEACHING FOR ENGLISH LEARNERS (DATELs)

Digital-age teaching for ELs (DATELs) is the outcome of our decade-long work with ELs and technology. This framework requires that we embrace the opportunities presented to us in remote and hybrid instructional models and reimagine our instructional strategies and technology integration to meet the evolving needs of ELs. The strategies, tools, and lesson seeds provided in this book are designed to help us create more student-centered, culturally responsive learning experiences for ELs. Figure 1.1 identifies the key features of DATELs and illustrates how a digital-age learning ecosystem for ELs will accomplish the following:

- Increase social interaction and engagement
- Provide authentic communication and contextually rich language practice
- Reduce the affective filter so that more learning can occur
- Support scaffolded instruction through digital tools and media
- Incorporate all six literacy skills (listening, speaking, reading, writing, viewing, and visually representing)
- Emphasize the 5 Cs for 21st-century ELs (critical thinking, communication, collaboration, creativity, and culture)

As we examine our pedagogical practices and the role that technology plays in the education of English learners, we must also critically examine the deep-rooted inequities in our schools and societies. In K–12 schools and higher education settings, educational inequities—including the digital divide—have intensified the call to action: We must provide ELs with full and equitable participation in in-person, remote, and hybrid instructional models. In this book, we present strategies, resources, and ready-to-use practices for ELs to ensure meaningful and intentional outcomes that include:

- Bridging the digital divide to ensure equitable access for ELs to all instructional resources, materials, and learning opportunities in a variety of settings;
- Presenting an approach to planning instruction for ELs that includes content, language, social-emotional learning, and technology integration;
- Applying culturally and linguistically responsive and sustaining pedagogy to all types of instructional models.

LEARNING BY DOING

Educators today are reimagining the concept of learning by doing in the digital age. Inquiry-based and project-based learning activities that require digital literacy have become a part of everyday instruction. These instructional models call for a reexamination of Bloom's taxonomy as it applies to 21st-century learning. Do you recall the six dimensions of Bloom's taxonomy?

FIGURE 1.1 ● DATELs

DATELs

Digital Age Teaching for English Learners

Authentic Communication & Contextually Rich Language Practice

AFFECTIVE FILTER

SOCIAL INTERACTION

RECEPTIVE SKILLS

LISTENING · READING · VIEWING

EXPRESSIVE SKILLS

SPEAKING · WRITING · VISUALLY REPRESENTING

The 5C's for 21st Century English Learners

Communication · Collaboration · Creativity · Critical Thinking · Culture

online resources

Available for download from **resources.corwin.com/DigitalAgeTeachingforELs**

Consider what happens in the 21st-century version that has turned Bloom's taxonomy literally upside down (see Figure 1.2). In this rendition by Wright (2012), the skills are inverted as students begin with creating, then move up the pyramid through evaluating, analyzing, applying, understanding, and finally, remembering. This flipped visual conceptualization of Bloom's emphasizes a learning-by-doing philosophy and starts with a process of investigation and engagement as opposed to starting with direct teaching, lectures, and rote memorization.

Flipping Bloom's taxonomy in order to enhance students' ability to access higher-order thinking is also the subject of research on retrieval practice (Argawal, 2019). Whereas traditional study methods focus on drilling to get information into students' heads, retrieval practice is an instructional strategy that is focused on helping students pull knowledge out of their heads through actively recalling information. Learning by doing and activating prior knowledge before introducing new information is essential to helping English learners develop and retain new concepts in the target language.

When we commit to transforming education for ELs—and for all students in the digital age—we also commit to a shift in priority from students as consumers of information to students as creators. For English learners, the emphasis on starting with creating and activating prior knowledge means engaging them

FIGURE 1.2 ● Bloom's 21

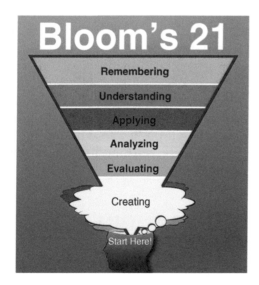

Source: https://shelleywright.wordpress.com/2012/05/29/flipping-bloomstaxonomy/

in authentic, communicative experiences and providing more opportunity to practice the target language. This is not "sink or swim" methodology! For these learning experiences to be productive, you need to lay down some groundwork. Indeed, the language required to participate in this type of learning is carefully scaffolded. We will explore how to accomplish this throughout the book.

An emphasis on student-centered, collaborative learning means increased opportunities for students to interact with peers and use English along with their full linguistic repertoires to complete authentic tasks. We must also emphasize the importance of using the SIX literacy domains (listening, speaking, reading, writing, viewing, and visually representing) to engage students in multimodal language, literacy, and disciplinary practices. You can engage ELs in this highly communicative environment by using carefully scaffolded questioning techniques that lead ELs to evaluate and analyze tasks. As a result, they develop higher-order thinking skills and use academic discourse across all content areas.

REMOTE AND HYBRID LEARNING ENVIRONMENTS

An integral part of the digital-age learning environment is the use of Flipped Learning methodologies (Bergman & Sams, 2012). There are many different versions of Flipped Learning and we have devoted a chapter to it along with its benefits for ELs later in this book. Flipped Learning methodology is neatly aligned to best practices for ELD/ESL instruction. Simply stated, in Flipped Learning environments, direct instruction moves from the group learning space to the individual learning space (flipped-learning.org). This creates more time for students to collaborate and create when they are together in person or virtually. With a combined understanding of Bloom's 21 and the Flipped Learning model, you will build a foundation for self-directed learning whether you are working in fully remote or hybrid classroom settings.

 UNDERSTANDING ELs

WHO ARE OUR ENGLISH LEARNERS?

Before we address the unique needs of ELs, let us take a snapshot of the U.S. EL population. English learners are considered a unique, ever-growing subgroup of the U.S. student population. According to Hussar et al. (2020):

- The population of students designated as English language learners (ELs) has increased from 3.8 million students (8.1%) in 2000 to 5 million (10.1%) in 2017, and it is estimated to continue to grow.

- Roughly 3 out of 4 ELs speak Spanish as their home language, whereas the next nine most common languages are Arabic, Chinese, Vietnamese, Somali, Russian, Portuguese, Haitian or Haitian Creole, and Hmong.

- The most newly identified subgroup of ELs attend kindergarten to 3rd grade.

- Approximately 15% of ELs are also identified as students with disabilities

- Only 2% of ELs are labeled as gifted.

When it comes to academic achievement measured by standardized assessment, there are numerous studies that report a substantial opportunity gap. For example, in 2019, "the reading score for 4th-grade ELL students was 33 points lower than the score for their non-ELL peers" (p. 73). In the same year, "the average mathematics score for 4th-grade ELL students was 24 points lower than the score for their non-ELL peers" (p. 84).

These facts certainly tell an evolving story, yet our suggestion is to seek out a much more personal story: in our day-to-day practice what is most important is to get to know each EL as an individual with unique characteristics, vast cultural heritages, complex academic and non-academic experiences, and rich linguistic repertoires.

How can we best respond to the diversity among this student population? Honigsfeld and Dove (2019) suggest that educators recognize and carefully address the complex variation that exists among ELs. It has been noted that ELs are far from being a homogenous group requiring a one-size-fits-all approach; instead, they may differ based on the following factors: (a) prior schooling, (b) level of language proficiency in the native tongue or in any additional languages, (c) level of literacy in languages other than English, (d) level of language proficiency in English, and (e) the student's learning trajectory. See Table 1.1 and reflect on which of these groups and subgroups of ELs you work with in your own school.

The purpose of this summary table is to alert you to the vast *within-group* diversity that you are likely to encounter when working with ELs and to offer a quick reference guide to the complex background experiences and readiness levels that are to be expected among ELs. The technology tools and practices we suggest will also have to be carefully selected, adjusted, or modified to best match the needs of ELs. To better understand the unique background experiences and cultural knowledge that ELs bring to the school, we as educators, must not only collaborate with each other and engage in ongoing professional learning opportunities, we can also reach out to the community both physically and virtually. Creating multilingual, interactive online resources for parents of ELs that identify what they need to know about enrolling their child and supporting their learning in an American school is an opportunity to build a trusting relationship and enhance parent engagement.

When English learners represent such complex subgroups as depicted in Table 1.1, you may find it overwhelming to learn

TABLE 1.1 ● Diversity Among English Language Learners

Prior education
• Formal, grade-appropriate education in another country
• Formal, grade-appropriate education in school system
• Interrupted formal, grade-appropriate education in another country
• Interrupted formal, grade-appropriate education in school system
Linguistic development in language(s) other than English
• Monolingual (home language only)
• Bilingual in two languages other than English
• Bidialectal speaking both a standard language other than English and a dialect
• Multilingual in three or more languages
Status of language proficiency and literacy in language(s) other than English
• Only receptive language skills
• Productive oral language skills
• Emerging literacy skills
• Grade-appropriate literacy skills
• Any or all of the above skills in more than one language other than English
Level of English language proficiency (WIDA, 2020)
1. Entering: Knows and uses minimal social language and minimal academic language with visual and graphic support

2.	Emerging: Knows and uses some social English and general academic language with visual and graphic support
3.	Developing: Knows and uses social English and some specific academic language
4.	Expanding: Knows and uses social English and some technical academic language
5.	Bridging: Knows and uses social English and academic language working with grade level material
6.	Reaching: Knows and uses social and academic language at the highest level

Learning trajectory

- Demonstrating typical academic and linguistic developmental trajectories

- Demonstrating academic and/or linguistic developmental challenges and difficulties that do not respond well to accelerated learning

- Demonstrating academic and/or linguistic developmental challenges and difficulties that respond well to systemic interventions

- Demonstrating academic and/or linguistic developmental challenges and difficulties that require special attention

Source: Adapted from Honigsfeld and Dove, 2015.

about and keep in mind each student's background information regarding the following key questions:

- If the student was born outside of the country are there any unusual circumstances or trauma surrounding the child's arrival to their new home? Is there sufficient information available about the child's previous educational background, and how can the transition to a new school system be as seamless as possible?

- What is the child's language proficiency and literacy level in the home language, in English, and in any additional languages?

- Are there any indications of gaps in education, learning difficulties, or other predictable challenges?

We suggest maintaining important information about the ELs in your school in a student management or learning management system that would allow you and your colleagues to have access to basic information about each EL. You can also create your own database by using Google Forms or a similar tool to survey your students individually using the profile template shown in Table 1.2. EL Portrait at a Glance

TABLE 1.2 ● EL Portrait at a Glance

Name:	Date:
Student Background/Social-Emotional Information:	
Student Academic Strengths:	Student Academic Needs:
Student Technology Strengths:	Student Technology Needs:
Language and Literacy Development Goals:	
Accommodations or Modifications: (if necessary)	

Source: Adapted from Honigsfeld and Dove, 2015.

MAKE-IT-YOUR-OWN LESSON SEEDS

As you explore the lesson seeds provided in this book consider how they may be adapted for use in your content area for your grade level and for your unique group of students. Also consider how these lesson seeds can be transformed into HyperDocs for student use. HyperDocs are online documents that contain content, links, and instructions for students to follow; they are designed to support self-directed learning. Students use the HyperDoc to guide them through an interactive learning experience by clicking on a highlighted word or image. HyperDocs can be shared with students in the same way any online document might be shared in your learning management systems (see more on HyperDocs in Chapter 2).

Each lesson seed accomplishes the following:

1. **Sets student goals that encompass multiliteracies and multimodalities**

   Learning targets allow students to understand what they are expected to learn and how to demonstrate what they have learned. As mentioned earlier, digital-age instruction must integrate core content, with technology and language targets that relate to real-world communication and collaboration. ELs must be empowered to take ownership of their learning and effectively develop communication skills for the classroom and beyond.

2. **Activates students' prior knowledge**

   Activating prior knowledge helps ELs make connections to new information and use higher-order thinking skills they are learning in the classroom. We can tap into what students already know by first assessing prior knowledge and skills and then making connections between the new concepts being taught and the students' knowledge and experiences. ELs whose funds of knowledge are not aligned to what is taught in U.S. schools greatly benefit from activities that explicitly build foundational skills and background information.

3. **Enhances student engagement**

   You can make content accessible for English learners by providing an environment in which students learn by doing. You can differentiate instruction through a blend of technology resources that provide multimodalities and entry points. ELs can then access the content and participate as active learners in the classroom. This approach to delivering instruction ensures that the lesson is comprehensible to students, and it meets the language demands of grade-level content. Including explicit instruction of academic language is important to the development of higher-order thinking processes associated with literacy and academic settings.

High levels of student engagement may be achieved through careful planning of learning activities that motivate students while also providing opportunities for frequent student-to-student interactions within the classroom. For ELs, activities should integrate all language domains (listening, speaking, reading, writing, viewing, and visually representing), as well as address digital literacy.

Here is a description of the categories in our lesson seed template. You can reproduce this template to create your own lessons:

[TITLE]

[Grade Level]

In this lesson students will…

Student Goals

- **I can [language target]**
- **I can [content target]**
- **I can [tech target]**

ACTIVATE

Activating prior knowledge and building background information is essential to help ELs engage with content in the target language

CREATE

Start with an inquiry process. Break activities into manageable steps according to the needs of each student. Allow students to engage in productive struggle and problem solving in order to create the targeted outcome.

EVALUATE & ANALYZE

Allow students to use critical thinking skills and to complete needs assessment and analyze findings to plan next steps

COLLABORATE & APPLY

Students work together and use what they have learned to complete an authentic task

DEMONSTRATE

Students show what they know by publishing, demonstrating or presenting product or outcome to an authentic audience

REFLECT, ASSESS & REMEMBER

Incorporate authentic assessment including peer review, audience feedback, journaling and self assessment rubrics to allow students to reflect on and remember what they have learned.

| **EXPAND** |
| Provide additional resources and activities for various proficiency levels to personalize instruction and provide opportunity for ELs to integrate the lesson content and newly acquired language skills. |

 Available for download from **resources.corwin.com/DigitalAgeTeachingforELs**

CONSIDER THIS

OPPORTUNITIES FOR COLLABORATION

One of the 5 Cs of 21st-century skills we discussed earlier is collaboration. As longtime collaborators, we believe that it is essential for educators to foster collaboration not only between students but also with other teachers in their learning community. As you read through the book, we invite you to identify opportunities for teacher collaboration and/or student collaboration related to the theme of each chapter.

SOCIAL-EMOTIONAL NEEDS AND BUILDING RESILIENCE

The 21st-century immigrant experience to the United States has been riddled with ferocious political debates, anti-immigrant sentiments, increased global crises—be it economic, political, or other—that pushed migrants and refugees to leave their countries and seek a new home. Educators are uniquely positioned to embrace immigrant families and foster students' social and emotional well-being in the classroom and the larger community. A recent OECD (2018) report cautions that

> ensuring that students with an immigrant background have positive well-being outcomes represents a significant challenge, because many immigrants or mixed-heritage students must overcome the adversities associated with displacement, socio-economic disadvantage, language barriers and the difficulty of forging a new identity all at the same time. (p. 5)

Families and their children who try to make a new life in the United States are already demonstrating resilience by virtue of overcoming many hardships, including trauma surrounding their relocation to a new land; further nurturing students' resilience is one way to ensure that they overcome adversities, develop a stronger sense of belonging, and have higher levels of motivation and lower levels of academic anxiety (Colorin Colorado, 2018). Throughout the book, consider how to achieve this.

CULTURALLY RESPONSIVE-SUSTAINING EDUCATIONAL PRACTICES

We recognize that all students bring tremendous strengths to their learning. To ensure that asset-based, rather than deficit-focused instructional and programmatic decisions are made on behalf of ELs, in this book we build upon a current Culturally Responsive-Sustaining Education (CR-SE) framework published by NYSED (2019). We chose this framework because it synthesizes the most current understandings about how to

> helps educators create student-centered learning environments that: affirm racial, linguistic and cultural identities; prepare students for rigor and independent learning, develop students' abilities to connect across lines of difference; elevate historically marginalized voices; and empower students as agents of social change. (para. 1)

More specifically, we advocate for technology integration for 21st-century learning experiences that

- recognize and proactively respond to the digital divide that exists among communities
- ensure equitable access to information, tools, and resources for ELs
- create a welcoming and affirming digital learning environment
- afford students an inclusive technology-supported curriculum
- match high rigor with high support for all

Our intention is to place special emphasis on culturally and linguistically responsive and sustaining pedagogy in each chapter to help leverage students' differential backgrounds, experiences, learning pathways, and trajectories as assets.

RESOURCES OUTSIDE THE SCHOOL CONTEXT

To better understand the unique background experiences and cultural knowledge that ELs bring to the school, we must not only collaborate with each other and engage in ongoing professional learning opportunities, we must also connect with the larger community both physically and virtually. Creating multilingual, interactive online resources for parents of ELs that identify what they need to know about enrolling their child and supporting their learning in school is an often-overlooked opportunity to enhance parent participation in their child's education. Such resources also open the door to more vibrant family and community engagement. Takanishi and Le Menestrel (2017) note that family engagement among EL parents may be expanded and enhanced when the following key practices are in place:

> creating a welcoming environment, providing orientation programs, using technology to enhance two-way communication, instituting district- and school-level parent advisory committees and school support teams that include parents of ELs to support ELs' academic success and emotional well-being, and instituting adult education programs for parents of ELs. (p. 281)

Which of these ideas resonate with you and could be considered in your context?

 DIGITAL-AGE EXPLORER'S CORNER

Each vignette in the following chapters is provided by teaching professionals who are currently working in the field. As you read about the learning experiences they have created for their students, imagine the possibilities of adopting similar instructional practices and leveraging technology tools in your own teaching context, for your own unique group of students.

Chapter Summary

- Creating a digital learning ecosystem in your classroom helps ELs communicate using multiple modalities and supports the development of multiliteracy skills.

- The DATELs framework incorporates the 5Cs: communication, collaboration, creativity, critical thinking, and culture into the six language domains: writing, speaking, visually representing, reading, listening, and viewing .

- Incorporating Flipped Learning with inquiry-based learning models allows ELs to access higher-order thinking skills and increases opportunities to use the target language.

- In order to meet the unique needs of each EL we must first understand the complex diversity of this subgroup of students.

- Culturally responsive education practices include addressing the digital divide that disproportionately affects ELs and their families.

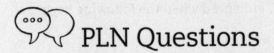 PLN Questions

1. What types of digital learning resources (DLRs) do you currently use with ELs in your school and why?

2. How does Bloom's 21 pertain to your classroom and the use of DLRs?

3. How can the DATELs framework guide instruction for ELs?

4. What resources can we offer families of English learners to support them in working with their children at home?

5. How can technology be used to make your classroom more culturally responsive and focus on students' cultural and linguistic knowledge?

CHAPTER 2

The Six Language Domains (Listening, Speaking, Reading, Writing, Viewing, and Visually Representing)

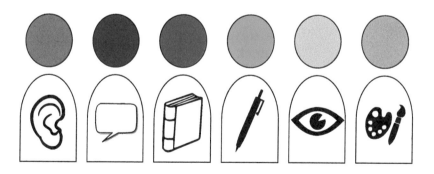

To achieve advanced literacies for all, especially in school settings characterized by linguistic diversity, leaders must work to create a cohesive literacy environment.

(Lesaux, 2016, p. 28)

OVERVIEW

In this chapter, we explore how to use digital learning resources (DLRs) to support and advance the acquisition of language and multiliteracies for ELs while also allowing ELs access to academic content in a whole new way. Every English teacher can identify the four language domains of listening, speaking, reading, and writing, but did you know that there are actually six language domains to include in our instruction? As early as 1996, viewing and visually representing were officially recognized as forms of literacy, and today the need to include viewing and visually representing in our teaching and language learning standards is more important than ever before (NCTE, 1996, WIDA 2020).

Digital learning resources can help to reduce language boundaries and promote literacy skills via all six language domains: listening, speaking, reading, writing, viewing, and visually representing. When used strategically, digital learning resources provide ELs with a multimodal experience while introducing new concepts and ideas. Presenting content in multiple ways helps ELs to retain information and reinforces vocabulary development, comprehension, and background knowledge.

This approach can also be helpful for "ever ELs" or former ELs (students who have been identified as English learners at any point during their enrollment in the school system) who typically no longer receive targeted services, although they may still need additional literacy and language support to reach proficiency in English. Hattie and Yates (2014) suggest that learning is a deliberate process—slow in pace; it does not often occur without sufficient time, focus, support, monitoring, and practice: "Impressions of quick learning are deceptive for many reasons. Unless the material is strongly meaningful, relevant and timely, it is subject to rapid and substantial forgetting ... To become skilled in a new area takes about 50 to 100 hours of practice" (p. 113).

When considering the language domains, digital learning resources allow for interactivity, and increased interest and engagement than more traditional formats. They also provide the repetition and reinforcement that all ELs need to gain academic language proficiency. Further, digital media can offer the much-needed, continued engagement with language that will yield higher levels of competence in English for ever ELs or former ELs.

🌐 DIGITAL-AGE LEARNING EXPERIENCE

English learners develop basic communication skills during day-to-day interactions with peers and teachers, but how do we support the development of the cognitive communicative skills needed to be successful in in-person, remote, or hybrid academic settings? Language used in a school setting (for example, a social studies text versus a science text) may challenge ELs as they learn core academic content. In addition, ELs may encounter difficulties when attempting to communicate their ideas using precise academic discourse. Digital media presentations could support the acquisition of content specific vocabulary and academic language since the use of digital media provides a low-anxiety environment that incorporates all six domains of listening, speaking, reading, writing, viewing, and visually representing. When students experience language development through digital media, they have multiple access points to content, they can express their ideas, and they interpret and represent concepts using multiple modalities while making connections to spoken and written language. (See Table 2.1 for examples how digital media may support the development of receptive and expressive skills.)

TABLE 2.1 ● Using Digital Media With ELs

USING DIGITAL MEDIA FOR RECEPTIVE SKILLS
Listening. Digital media offers English learners the opportunity to listen to authentic language with the ability to control the rate and to pause and repeat the listening activity. ELs can listen to language lessons, story read-alouds, news reports, interviews, and a wide variety of podcasts at any grade level and in multiple languages to experience the target language in context. Platforms like Wonderopolis, News-o-matic, and Podbean provide various listening opportunities for students.
Reading. English learners can use electronic texts and e-books to interpret and relate information to their own personal experiences. Online digital resources such as Newsela, TumbleBooks, and Common Lit provide information to ELs at a reading level that's right for them.
Viewing. Viewing requires skills similar to reading comprehension for English Learners. Viewing can include everything from images to video presentations. Instructional videos, images and resources found in platforms such as Discovery Education, Khan Academy, TedED, and YouTube provide multiple modalities for ELs to gain understanding of concepts.
USING DIGITAL MEDIA FOR EXPRESSIVE SKILLS
Speaking. English learners can express thoughts and ideas clearly and effectively using various forms of digital media to communicate orally. Students can record their own podcasts, provide audio feedback to peers and narrate digital stories by making use of tools like GarageBand, Anchor, Kaizena, and Ed.VoiceThread.

(Continued)

TABLE 2.1 ● (Continued)

Writing. English learners can communicate through print by using digital learning resources in everyday writing tasks. Students can be authors of e-books, class websites, and blogs. Students can practice writing skills in a more supportive and low-anxiety environment in mediated social networking chats with peers. Platforms such as Storybird, Weebly, Edublogs, and Twitter facilitate writing and collaboration.

Visually Representing. This form of communication requires English Learners to collect and organize information, decide on the best way to convey it to others, and produce a visual product to accomplish this communication, often incorporating print and sound (including speech) with the visual images. Tools such as Screencastify, ThingLink, Educreations, and Powtoon facilitate communication through the use of visual imagery.

REMOTE AND HYBRID LEARNING ENVIRONMENTS

To reinforce the explicit connection between content and language acquisition for ELs in the digital-age classroom, the WIDA ELD Standards Framework (2020) emphasizes the importance of multimodality. Using multimodal resources creates a flexible learning environment that promotes student engagement and expression. Remote and hybrid learning environments provide us with such flexibility while also promoting self-directed learning. When we design instruction for ELs in both remote and hybrid learning environments, we must be mindful to break activities into concrete steps using digital resources that incorporate the six language domains we have described in this chapter.

Whether delivering instruction in a hybrid or remote model, you can assign differentiated asynchronous learning tasks to respond to individual student needs and provide targeted reinforcement of concepts during synchronous instructional time. Since digital media supports differentiated instructional practices that increase receptive and expressive skills, it gives both you and your students more opportunities for reflection and feedback. English proficiency should not be considered a prerequisite for participation in content learning. Digital resources provide scaffolds and tools to overcome language barriers while making content comprehensible.

When designing learning activities for remote and hybrid instruction refer to the framework provided by Hobbs (2011), which identifies multiliteracy skills required for students in the digital age:

1. ACCESS. Finding and sharing appropriate and relevant information and using media texts and technology tools well.

2. ANALYZE. Using critical thinking to analyze message purpose, target audience, quality, veracity, credibility, point of view, and potential effects or consequences of messages.

3. CREATE. Composing or generating content using creativity and confidence in self-expression, with awareness of purpose, audience, and composition techniques.

4. REFLECT. Considering the impact of media messages and technology tools upon our thinking and actions in daily life and applying social responsibility and ethical principles to our own identity, communication behavior, and conduct.

5. ACT. Working individually and collaboratively to share knowledge and solve problems in the family, the workplace, and the community, and participating as a member of a community at local, regional, national, and international levels. (p. 12)

This instructional model aligns seamlessly with the International Society for Technology in Education Standards for Students ISTE 1a-d (2017)

1. Empowered Learner

Students leverage technology to take an active role in choosing, achieving, and demonstrating competency in their learning goals, informed by the learning sciences.

 UNDERSTANDING ELs

The gateway to academic engagement is academic language. Among others, Schleppegrell (2012) observed, "Academic language is functional for getting things done at school, varying as it is used in different subject areas and for different purposes, but requiring that children use language in new ways to learn and to display knowledge about what they have learned in ways that will be valued" (p. 410). Academic language is frequently conceptualized as having three dimensions: a word dimension, a sentence dimension, and a text dimension (WIDA, 2020). These dimensions, earlier referred to as levels, are not to be seen as isolated learning targets; rather, they are reminders of the important features of English that ELs need exposure to and ample opportunity to practice and master. See Table 2.2 for a summary of the three academic language dimensions' distinct features, challenges (also seen as *opportunities*) ELs face as they work on mastering them, and key instructional practices for classroom use.

TABLE 2.2 ● Academic Language Dimensions, Features, Challenges, and Essential Instructional Practices

DIMENSION	ACADEMIC LANGUAGE FEATURES	CHALLENGES FOR ELs	ESSENTIAL INSTRUCTIONAL PRACTICES
Word (Vocabulary or Phrases)	Generic academic terms	Volume of vocabulary needed	Exposure to vast vocabulary through interactions with language-rich texts
	Discipline-specific academic terms	Nuances of word meanings	An interactive environment in which verbal exchanges are encouraged not silenced
	Figurative and idiomatic expressions	Phrases and collocations	Word learning strategies
	Words with multiple meanings		
	Roots and affixes		
Sentence	Sentence structure	Complex sentences with low-frequency words	Sentence dissection
	Sentence length		
	Grammatical structures		Scaffolded sentence frames
	Pronouns	Advanced grammatical features (passive voice, participles)	Mentor text
	Context Clues		
	Proverbs		
Text or Discourse	Text organization	Reading and lexile levels	Genre study
	Text craft and structure	Complexity of ideas	Read-alouds
			Shared reading
			Scaffolded independent reading
	Text density	Background knowledge needed for comprehension	Inquiry groups
	Clarity and coherence	Styles and structures unique to each genre or text type	Text analysis
	Text types and genres		Text annotation

Source: Adapted from Pritchard and O'Hara, 2016; Honigsfeld and Dove, 2021; WIDA, 2020.

Using complex academic language in and outside the classroom goes beyond teaching words, practicing sentence structures, and reading and responding to increasingly complex texts. It involves students' learning to process and internalize new skills and information while also engaging in emerging language use to communicate. For language to develop in a systemic way, ELs must be listening, speaking, reading, writing, viewing, and visually representing authentically in their new language every day. Researchers and practitioners whose work is informed by sociocultural theory also believe that language acquisition and literacy learning happen when "knowledge and understanding are co-constructed through interaction, and through the practice of scaffolding, whereby the learner's understandings and attempts to express these in words are supported and assisted through dialogue" (Cullen et al., 2013, p. 426).

Consider the following listening and speaking strategies to encourage a more complex academic dialogue for ELs:

- Employ scaffolded "talk moves." Give your students appropriate sentence stems for various common language functions. Help them learn to ask for clarification when they do not understand something (Would you explain what ____ means?); paraphrase someone else's idea (What I heard you say is ____); extend what a classmate said (In addition to what ____ said,); or agree or disagree with others (I agree with ____ /I respectfully disagree with ____).

- Provide productive wait time that includes a quick write or quick draw. Students gather their thoughts, jot down some ideas, and enter the academic conversation feeling better prepared.

- Elicit longer answers from ELs who are at a more advanced language proficiency level. Invite students to elaborate on their short answers by encouraging them to give some examples, add more details, describe a person or object they mentioned, or explain their thinking further.

- Use flexible grouping configurations that include whole-group teacher-led discussion sessions, small-group interactions, cooperative learning groups, triads, and pairs.

Key research-based reading strategies that support ELs include the following:

- Conduct frequent formative assessments of ELs' reading development, such as how well they demonstrate letter-sound correspondence; letter recognition; word-, sentence-, and text-level reading comprehension; and fluency. Based on data, support ELs in the areas most needed and monitor their progress over time.

- Focus on Tier One and Tier Two vocabulary to address the meaning of everyday conversational phrases, idioms, and expressions that may cause confusion, as well as high-frequency, Tier Three academic words.

- Ask carefully constructed questions before, during, and after reading to support ELs' reading comprehension. Ask for literal responses that require students to recall factual information or readily available details. Probe them to offer their interpretations of what was read as well as engage in critical reflection, analysis, and application of the new information read.

- Read aloud to students and model comprehension strategies you use through thinking aloud or comprehending aloud (Zwiers, 2014). Allow students to gain insight into your reading comprehension process. When they hear what you did when you came across a certain word, how you interpreted the actions of a certain character, or how you made sense of a new piece of information in a nonfiction selection, they will see these examples as models of literacy actions they can emulate.

- Consider how to support ELs while they engage in the three levels of meaning making and comprehension as outlined by Willingham (2017): "we extract ideas from sentences, we connect the ideas across sentences, and we build a general idea of what a text is about" (p. 126).

For ELs to develop writing skills, we need to make writing a daily occurrence. Dorfman and Cappelli (2017) also advocate for the study of exemplary written work such as mentor texts through which ELs can better understand what constitutes accomplished writing. Wolsey and his colleagues (2010) claim that "all students are to act and believe that literacy is valued and valuable" (p. 10). Students can achieve this goal only if they experience the collective sense of importance literacy holds for them individually and for the entire school community collectively. When you and your colleagues collaborate to plan academic language learning and literacy development activities that meaningfully connect with each other, ELs can make better sense of the patterns in language and literacy.

Key writing strategies we suggest include the following:

- Invite recently arrived ELs with high levels of literacy skills in their home language to write in that language. They can add illustrations or English-language labels that support their writing. As English proficiency grows, ask them to collaborate and create a wiki glossary of key ideas, an outline or bulleted list, or a brief summary in a classroom English blog.

- Provide writing scaffolds such as word boxes, sentence stems, paragraph frames, or essay outlines as needed.

- Use bilingual peer bridges, teaching assistants, and print and electronic dictionaries. Use resources like Google slides to create bilingual glossaries to connect literacy in the home language with that of the new language.

- Introduce and maintain a variety of daily writing tasks such as digital Quick Write prompts that will activate students' prior knowledge and engage ELs in brief forms of response writing in response to a topic or text.

- Adapt the writing process to the needs of ELs by spending more time on prewriting, drafting, and editing; structuring writing tasks into shorter, more manageable subtasks; and using shared online documents to post written and/or audio feedback to guide students through each step with questions and prompts, step-by-step directions, and modeling, as well as samples and exemplars.

- Support writing with visuals, digital mind-mapping, diagrams, word banks, glossaries, lists of words, outlines, or templates as needed.

Similarly, when students engage in viewing or visually representing their understanding, they have authentic opportunities to interact with complex ideas (e.g., watch a lecture on TED-Ed), develop new skills (watch someone model an artistic technique), experience extracurricular learning or extensions and enrichments to the core curriculum (go on a virtual field trip to a Smithsonian Museum, take a virtual tour of a gallery), participate in discipline-specific academic practices (complete a virtual frog dissection).

Key strategies that support viewing or visually representing new learning include the following:

- Select multilingual digital materials
- Turn on subtitles in English or the home language when available
- Use translation/interpretation apps
- Chunk viewing tasks to ensure time for meaning making via a stop-and-process protocol
- Embed comprehension checks and teacher notes into viewing assignments

MAKE-IT-YOUR-OWN LESSON SEEDS

The following brief overview provides a lesson topic with "seed" ideas that we invite you to "grow" into a full lesson plan for your classroom. The template may be adapted for use as a HyperDoc for student use.

STUDENT ADVOCACY GRADES 3–5

In the following lesson seed, students will employ their working knowledge and understanding of the concepts of citizenship, power, authority, and governance. Students will then use technology to locate the U.S. Capitol and other national buildings on Google Earth. Students will participate in a virtual reality field trip to the White House, and take verbal or pictorial notes during their experiential learning. Virtual field trips provide online access to many locations that your class may not get a chance to visit on their own. Students can explore many locations and discover extraordinary places just by using online virtual trip resources. They also eliminate logistical barriers such as time and money that traditional field trips require and provide more equitable access to a variety of learning experiences. After the field trip, students may work in groups to identify a problem in their community that might be resolved through legislation and use Twitter to advocate for the legislation.

STUDENT GOALS

- **I can** describe the functions of state governments and define *capital* as the location of state and national government and *capitol* as the building in which government is located.

- **I can** identify the nation's capital on a map and name the major national buildings and sites in Washington, D.C.

- **I can** use Google Earth to locate the U.S. Capitol and other national buildings. I can participate in a virtual reality tour of the White House

ACTIVATE

Students review the formation of the United States with an emphasis on citizenship, government, and economics. Students read or view information about how a bill becomes a law.

CREATE

Students identify a problem in their community that might be resolved through legislation. Create a public service announcement (PSA) about a key issue and post it in Flipgrid.

EVALUATE & ANALYZE

Students review all Flipgrid posts, compare notes, and select one topic to use to propose a new law for the community.

COLLABORATE & APPLY

In groups, students write a proposal for the new law.

Create a hashtag (#) for the proposal to connect group members on Twitter and Tweet ideas about the community issue and the proposed legislation, include pictures, videos, and links about the community based on your research.

DEMONSTRATE

Students present their proposed legislation during a virtual or in-person mock assembly.

REFLECT, ASSESS, & REMEMBER

Students use a peer-review rubric to assess the proposed legislation with an emphasis on citizenship, government, and economics.

EXPAND

Use Google Earth to search places and navigate street views of Washington, D.C. Participate in a virtual reality tour of the White House using the Google Arts and Culture app. https://artsandculture.google.com/partner/the-white-house. Add hyperlinks to more activities and online resources to expand and differentiate the learning experience based on student needs.

CONSIDER THIS

OPPORTUNITIES FOR COLLABORATION

Language and literacy develop when students participate in authentic opportunities to interact with complex learning materials and express themselves in a variety of ways. Previously, we advocated for a SWIRL-ing classroom, one in which students speak, write, interact, read, and listen while constructing new knowledge, practicing emerging skills, and making meaning collaboratively. Let's go a few steps further and make sure multimodal, multiliteracy experiences are provided not only during designed ELD classes or courses but across all core content areas as well as the special subject areas for ELs. One way to achieve this is collaboration.

RESPONDING TO SOCIAL-EMOTIONAL NEEDS-BUILDING RESILIENCE

Have you ever heard a fellow educator state that working with ELs is just good teaching? We have! Hopkins and her colleagues (2019) offer us an explanation for this commonly heard misconception, and we invite you to share this response with your colleagues: it is a "misconception that overlooks the nature of language development and its relationship to content learning, and obscures attention to ELs' sociocultural and social-emotional experiences" (p. 2301). Developing oracy and literacy and engaging in multilingual, multimodal, digitally supported learning experiences may carry special challenges and rewards. Commit to providing ELs with joyful learning opportunities to participate in all domains (speaking, listening, reading, writing, viewing, and visually interpreting) with growing confidence. While doing so, ELs may also develop tolerance for ambiguity, risk-taking skills, and perseverance to overcome perceived or actual obstacles. One way to achieve that is to balance student participation in these domains at the independent versus instructional levels.

CULTURALLY RESPONSIVE-SUSTAINING EDUCATIONAL PRACTICES

Culturally responsive-sustaining pedagogy is closely related to critical literacy, which "positions teachers and learners as co-constructors of knowledge" (Bacon, 2017, p. 425) and focuses on *reading the word and the world* (Freire & Macedo, 1987). As such, it helps students critically analyze texts in all genres as well produce new understandings about the complex cultural and social experiences including social inequities in one's local and global community. We have adapted Bacon's (2017) framework on critical literacy in English language teaching (ELT) to expand it to culturally responsive and sustaining critical digital literacy by acknowledging that ELs experience language and literacy development in the six domains across three potentially overlapping processes

1. *Incidental language and literacy learning*: ELs participate in self-directed or peer-supported language and literacy practices that lead to authentic discoveries about the world with all its historical and contemporary complexities and inequities.

2. *Explicit language and literacy learning*: ELs participate in teacher-directed or teacher-facilitated instruction that focuses on critical analysis of historical, social, and cultural concepts, conditions, and issues.

3. *Integrated language and literacy learning*: ELs participate in teacher-directed and authentic learning opportunities that are purposefully infused; content, language, literacy, and critical thinking are integrated with intention and consistency to ensure development in all areas.

RESOURCES OUTSIDE THE SCHOOL CONTEXT

When we recognize that English learners and their families already engage in a range of oracy and literacy practices in multiple languages, including storytelling, reading environmental print, watching television shows, playing video games, reading and viewing for enjoyment, we also recognize that resources that are available in the home (computers with internet access, books, newspapers, magazines) and the community (libraries, after-school programs and clubs) may serve as rich sources of materials for exploration. At the same time, it is critical to address inequities in resources and provide much needed print- and technology-based tools to families who cannot afford them. Further, parents must have information in the language accessible to them regarding what their children are expected to learn in school and how they can support such learning at home.

Which of these ideas resonate with you and could be considered in your context?

 DIGITAL-AGE EXPLORER'S CORNER

BUILDING LANGUAGE CAPACITY FOR ELs

KATIE DIGREGORIO, WEST HEMPSTEAD UNION FREE SCHOOL DISTRICT

Language is not a barrier; engagement is achievable for all learners. The goal of instructional technology is to allow students to make a meaningful connection with the content. At the West

Hempstead Union Free School District, we use instructional technology to provide differentiated, individualized, and highly engaging lessons. The ENL (English as a New Language) teachers apply various instructional technology tools to meet students where they are in language acquisition and allow them to acquire the content knowledge to be successful. The purpose of the instructional technology for our EL students is to enable them to build language capacity in both the academic and social constructs and navigate the digital world beyond the classroom environment.

Our teachers also use various instructional technology tools to curate their reading and writing in the workshop model. For example, in elementary classrooms, students publish their written works using Book Creator and then record themselves reading aloud. Additionally, the teachers use Seesaw in the primary grades to have students practice phonics and sight words to build foundational literacy. The instructional technology elevated the work products from the readers' and writers' workshop, which allowed the EL students to build grade-level academic literacy. At the elementary level, the ENL teachers use these tools to facilitate language development and not simply deliver the instruction. The technology tools selected are purposeful and appropriate for the readers' and writers' workshop goals.

At the middle level, the teachers use Thinglink, Book Creator, and the HyperDoc model of instruction to build background knowledge and individualize instruction. The students can participate in the lessons no matter their language acquisition level and are producing work that reflects this intentional use of instructional technology. The students work in groups using Google Meet breakout rooms and programs such as Padlet and Nearpod. They can collaborate, critically think, and communicate with fellow ELs and their English proficient peers. At the high school level, a significant focus of our district is on project-based learning. The district provides professional development from the Buck Institute (PBLworks.org). In the 2020–2021 school year, in place of traditional mid-year assessments, the high school ELs—with the Buck Institute student choice and agency framework—created projects that showed their understanding of complex scientific phenomena and mathematical concepts. The students used "mock Tik-Tok templates" from *Ditch that Textbook* (Miller, 2019), Google Forms to collect data, and the Kami app to graph the data. Students at varying levels of language proficiency were able to showcase their understanding of Regents level material at a pace and space that met their needs. The passing rate for the ELs who participated in PBL was 80%.

Chapter Summary

- The six language domains are listening, speaking, reading, writing, viewing, and visually representing.

- Digital media supports both receptive and expressive academic language skills for ELs.

- ELs experience language and literacy development in the six domains across three potentially overlapping processes: incidental, explicit, and integrated language and literacy learning.

- When we design instruction for ELs for in-person, remote and hybrid learning environments we must be mindful to break activities into concrete steps using digital resources that incorporate the six language domains.

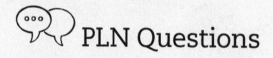 # PLN Questions

1. How can digital learning resources support real and authentic language for in-person, remote, and hybrid instructional models?

2. Are you currently using digital learning resources? If so, how?

3. How can you use instructional videos to support all six language domains?

4. In what ways can you provide a more supportive and low-anxiety environment for ELs to express and support their receptive and expressive skills?

5. Describe how students can use digital media to demonstrate what they have learned.

6. Describe types of professional development that can transform pedagogy to enhance digital-age learning experiences for ELs?

CHAPTER 3

Critical Thinking and Assessment

Learners need endless feedback more than they need endless teaching.

(Wiggins, 2012, para. 2)

OVERVIEW

In this chapter we'll explore the way by which we promote critical thinking in our classroom through the use of assessment. The digital-age learning environment can help us transform traditional assessment of English learners into an assets-based model that better informs instruction and more accurately reflects academic progress. It is essential that the monitoring of progress for ELs is equitable and that data is used to inform instruction and student placement. We need to ensure that our school districts implement valid and reliable grading practices that are free from bias. Fair assessment includes the use of multiple modalities and encompasses formal assessments, project-based learning, and instructional activities that allow students to demonstrate their content knowledge and language skills. Authentic assessment methods created for the benefit of ELs should include modifications and accommodations that take into account language proficiency levels. We know that assessment of learning should be an ongoing process throughout the year. The ultimate goal is to receive input on the student's relative performance, to improve and monitor student learning, and to receive ongoing feedback in order to improve instructional practices.

The transition from a traditional classroom model to a digital-age classroom raises questions about how standardized assessments can yield information about a student's progress that's comparable to the 21st-century education that many students, including ELs, are receiving. The "opt-out/refusal movement" has gained momentum and many educators and parents are questioning the validity of administering standardized tests. For ELs, the issue is not only whether or not a test is valid or narrows curriculum, but whether or not we are creating culturally responsive learning institutions. According to Starr (2021), issues concerning equity of resources, racism, poverty, and organizing school systems to improve effectiveness are the core issues for discussion. Under the Every Student Succeeds Act, "states must use data from the exams to determine whether students are English proficient. Not offering the tests could hold back some students who are ready to exit English-learner status" (Mitchell, 2020). The ongoing debate about standardized testing by various stakeholders is not over. However, it highlights the need to design authentic skills-based assessment that monitors progress for ELs participating in both in-person and remote settings.

The digital-age learning environment shifts the culture of preparing students for standardized assessments to preparing assessments based on learning experiences within the classroom. An essential element of a digital-age learning ecosystem is creating a feedback loop for students. Hattie (2009) suggests, "The teacher provides supportive feedback and helps students to learn by acknowledging and using the student's prior knowledge and experiences, and monitoring to check if students know what is being taught, what is to be learnt, or what is to be produced" (p. 6). The digital-age learning environment ensures that ELs have authentic learning experiences, digital tools that promote student learning, and multiple ways to show their success in the classroom. When we design assessments that incorporate the use of technology, ELs have more ways to demonstrate mastery of a learning goal and more ways to experience success.

DIGITAL-AGE LEARNING EXPERIENCE

CREATING AUTHENTIC ASSESSMENTS

When designing instruction within your digital-age learning ecosystem "think out of the box." Look forward, identify future learning goals for your linguistically diverse students, and then plan your assessment first. This not only encompasses the basic premise of backward design introduced by Grant and McTighe (2005) but also emphasizes the principles of the Universal Design for Learning (UDL) Framework. #UDL Rising to Equity is a new initiative to update the UDL guidelines in order to "help any learning community identify, name, and redress systemic barriers to equitable learning and outcomes" (CAST, 2020, Oct. 6). Designing equitable and fair assessments for ELs is an important part of this mission. To meet this challenge, incorporate technology tools that help measure the student's ability to perform a task. Consider language proficiency levels and target a specific a learning outcome. Assessments that incorporate digital learning resources allow ELs to show what they know and what they have accomplished. Authentic assessments can be differentiated for independent study or may be a collaborative effort. This includes student collaboration through project-based learning, multimedia presentations for targeted audiences, and other authentic community experiences. Collaboration within a digital-age classroom promotes a culture of critical thinking, inquiry, and discovery. Shared learning gives students an opportunity to engage in discussion and take responsibility for their own learning, thus becoming critical thinkers (Totten et al., 1991). When the right technology tool is integrated into content-rich, collaborative learning activities and assessments, it provides multisensory access to that content, facilitating comprehension and allowing ELs to participate more effectively in academic discourse. Digital learning resources can be used to scaffold assessments that may otherwise be challenging for ELs due to the linguistic demands. In addition, using these tools to deliver content and assess student performance enhances traditional methods of delivery that are largely text based. This opens up the door to critical thinking by lowering the language barrier and channeling the instructional focus to academic content.

Video discussion platforms like Flipgrid can be used to integrate authentic assessment into classroom lessons. Flipgrid encourages ELs to practice organizing their thoughts and encourages classroom interaction and communication by having students post video responses to classroom Grid topics. The videos serve as a record for assessing student content knowledge and language skills. Students can create speaking rubrics that allow them to have a voice in the assessment process and develop an understanding of the expectations of the Flipgrid assignment.

Even traditional comprehension checks can be infused with technology to quickly make learning more visible. Google forms or online polling applications, such as Kahoot!, Socrative, or Quizziz, provide insight into levels of understanding among students and inform instruction to better meet the needs of English learners. When using this approach, participation becomes inclusive for all levels of English learners by lowering the affective variables that can negatively influence motivation, self-confidence, and anxiety within the classroom (Krashen, 2014). Online polling tools and opportunities to survey the class ensure that each student has a voice. Instead of relying on teacher-directed activities and formal assessments, focus on instructional time that provides fun, quick, and easy access to evaluate and inform instruction and identify the support needed for struggling learners. With technology you can add interactive activities to your lesson and collect student input no matter where your students are located, whether the session is synchronous or asynchronous. By leveraging the power of digital learning resources, you can give students immediate feedback and make formative assessment data collection a seamless part of everyday lessons.

Virtual collaboration boards like Padlet, Jamboard, and mind-mapping tools like Popplet can also offer immediate feedback on student progress. Students can easily share their thoughts or ideas with the class by posting text, images, links, or videos on the virtual wall to answer open-ended questions, extend discussions, and share their viewpoints. Tools like ExitTicket allow students to quickly and easily demonstrate what they've retained at the end of a lesson.

Authentic assessments afford ELs opportunities to develop ideas and freely participate in the classroom. The focus of authentic assessments is on student performance and the process and quality of the student's work. Many school districts are incorporating digital portfolios into their classrooms to allow students voice and choice in the assessment of their learning process. Digital portfolios allow for more self-directed learning and collaboration among teachers, students, and parents. Digital portfolios or e-portfolios give students voice and choice in their learning. Students select work products that they feel best represent their learning. Digital portfolios capture and share students' academic and creative development, provide opportunities for student reflection, and gather authentic information to improve students' learning process and progress. Seesaw is such a digital portfolio that empowers ELs to document their learning in a variety of ways. Students can insert images, videos, drawings, text, links, and voice recordings that are then accessible to teachers and parents. Any text written in Seesaw (like notes, captions, comments, announcements, or messages) can be translated in over 55 languages by both teachers and students' families. Seesaw gives ELs a safe space to practice so they have the confidence to attempt to complete tasks, make mistakes, reflect on their progress, and revise their work. In this capacity Seesaw helps capture the learning process, not just the end result.

Digital learning resources that are used for assessment not only allow us to gather data to inform instruction, they may also provide additional learning support, and even help us to communicate with parents. A communication platform such as ClassDojo helps teachers assess and monitor student behaviors, provide positive reinforcement and share student progress information with parents in real time.

Many English learners struggle with demonstrating their learning through traditional methods. For ELs, proficiency in reading and writing limits their participation within the classroom. By using digital learning resources in assessment, you can monitor and gauge the skills students have developed based on their performance. For instance, a blog can be used to encourage ELs to read and write in a positive forum that motivates students to read and respond and encourages group participation. Blogs can be used for assessment purposes in several ways. By posing questions and discussions among students, ELs can share their thoughts and ideas without the intimidation of having to speak in front of a class. Writing blog entries allow students to respond to or reflect on a topic. Maintaining a class website that includes a blog makes student learning visible and teacher expectations transparent. Blogging transforms the way information is shared to in-person, hybrid, and remote students and enhances the conversation to build relationships and cultivate an online classroom community. Blogging is a great language learning tool to provide a real audience for ELs writing. Blogs also provide additional reading practice which fosters feelings of community that promote discussion between students when posting comments on each other's blogs. Many blogging websites may or may not require a special log-in protocol, depending on the level of privacy you wish to establish. Blogs can be used as an extension to the learning that takes place in class, as well as serve as a link between home and school.

REMOTE AND HYBRID LEARNING ENVIRONMENTS

All educators must be prepared and knowledgeable in the effective implementation of remote and hybrid instruction in order to properly educate and assess students who may need additional support and scaffolding in online learning environments. We should employ multiple ways to measure student progress and create authentic methods for assessments in virtual learning. Tucker (2020) writes, "At its core, blended learning is a shift in control from teacher to learner. The goal of the various blended learning models is to give students more agency over the time, place, pace, and path of their learning" (p. 12).

Consider the following five strategies described by Tucker (2020), to help English learners reflect on learning and use language to self-assess and develop metacognition in your remote and hybrid classroom.

Students can use various digital learning resources to complete the following:

1. Plan and articulate their learning goals.

2. Complete learning logs and guided daily reflections.

3. Describe weekly what was learned and how it was learned.

4. Create Think-aloud video reflections.

5. Track and monitor their own progress.

This instructional model aligns seamlessly with the International Society for Technology in Education Standards for Students ISTE 3. a–d (2017).

3. Knowledge Constructor

Students critically curate a variety of resources using digital tools to construct knowledge, produce creative artifacts and make meaningful learning experiences for themselves and others.

 UNDERSTANDING ELs

ASSESSMENT PRACTICES AND ELs

In a recent report, Villegas and Pompa (2020) describe tremendous inconsistencies across the state policies regarding criteria for EL identification, reclassification, and inclusion into state accountability systems. It is beyond the scope of this book to address such complexities and challenges; instead, our focus is on day-to-day assessment practices that help inform instruction. Gottlieb (2021) presents a unique framework that describes assessment for ELs from three perspectives.

1. *Assessment as learning* suggests that English learners can meaningfully contribute to the assessment process. Through self-assessment and reflection, ELs develop agency and become more self-directed, independent learners, who can do the following:

   a. Learn to set their own goals

   b. Monitor and reflect on their progress

   c. Make choices of assessment task projects when offered

   d. Develop and maintain a student portfolio

   e. Participate in the assessment process in many other ways

2. *Assessment for learning* refers to the process that both classroom teachers and ELD/ESL specialists may employ on a regular basis. You can collect evidence of the learning targets your students have mastered, those they are in the process of mastering, and those they have yet to attain. Assessment for learning is primarily formative in nature, and as such, it helps inform instruction and offer feedback to students. Based on the formative assessment data collected, you may make adjustments to your teaching immediately or plan on reteaching a given skill or concept the following class session. Heritage (2011) notes that "teacher feedback is most beneficial when it assists students to understand their current learning status and provides hints, suggestions, or cues for them to act on. It is this, rather than offering general praise or total solutions, that enables students to assume a degree of responsibility for their learning" (p. 18).

3. *Assessment of learning* refers to processes that yield summative assessment data, including standardized testing. Nontraditional performance-based or

project-based assessments encourage learners to demonstrate what they have learned in creative ways, often allowing for the use of multiple modalities rather than responding to a traditional pencil and paper test.

Although differentiating instruction for ELs is becoming widely accepted and practiced, when it comes to assessment, some teachers might continue to assign identical projects and give identical quizzes and tests. We believe in collaboration not only to differentiate instruction but to design differentiated assessment tools as well. Honigsfeld and Dove (2019) suggest that co-assessment is a crucial, yet often overlooked, element of the collaborative instructional cycle that also includes co-planning, co-delivering instruction, and reflection on one's teaching. Technology-based tools such as Google Forms are ideal for progress monitoring and sharing information about ELs. When collaborating, you and your collaborators have editing rights to the (codeveloped) form and can have access to the data collected by each team member. Collaborative data collection and analysis help set consistent goals for ELs as well as support a more integrated approach to serving ELs.

Frey, Hattie, and Fisher (2018) suggest nurturing assessment-capable learners, who excel when conditions for learning are characterized by skill, will and thrill.

> Learners need to be equipped with the skills and knowledge, but also with the will to learn—this is the motivational component. When you combine skill and will, the result is the thrill of learning. It's the disposition that drives learners to investigate, explore, and take academic risks. (p. 10)

We, too, advocate for creating a learning environment in which students know how to assume responsibility for their learning: they can articulate what they are supposed to be learning and how far along they are on the path to mastery. They can track their own progress and set goals for themselves. This is especially important for ELs who need to develop into self-directed, independent learners.

Another critical dimension of assessment is considering the unique learning needs ELs may exhibit. ELs may either be underrepresented or overrepresented in special educational services but tend to be underrepresented in specially designed programs for gifted and talented students. One reason for these patterns is the limitations presented by tools and measures educators use during the identification process. ELs with exceptional needs (be it a learning disability, a language learning disorder, or giftedness) have to be supported to reach their full potential academically, linguistically, and socially. A key approach to teaching and assessing these youngsters is to focus on their strengths rather than taking a deficit-oriented approach. This way we can maximize their opportunity to build on their strengths and make progression with their language and literacy development and the core curriculum.

We firmly believe in and advocate for recognizing that emerging English fluency does not indicate a lack of academic potential. Just the contrary, with the right amount and types of supports and scaffolds, all ELs can make reasonable progressions and succeed in and out of school.

MAKE-IT-YOUR-OWN LESSON SEEDS

The following brief overview provides a topic with "seed" ideas that we invite you to "grow" into a full learning experience for your students whether in a remote, hybrid, or in-person classroom setting. The template can also be made into a HyperDoc for students to use.

ART AROUND THE WORLD GRADES 6–12

This lesson seed idea takes students on an Internet scavenger hunt using QR codes to guide them to various websites. They will research famous artists and explore resources such as the Google Cultural Institute and Google Art Project. After completing their research, students will create a student art gallery using the website Artsonia. Each group will focus on a different art movement and must write reflections about the artwork that affirm the racial, linguistic, and cultural identities of the artists. This project allows English learners to think critically about their work and use academic vocabulary to reflect on other students' work as well as their own. Together students will go on virtual tours to visit museums from around the world. They will work collaboratively to create their own gallery exhibit. They will create their own artwork reflective of the art movement and will write a short reflection on the piece. Digital learning resources such as QR codes, collaborative documents, and photo editors will be incorporated into the project. Visitors to the gallery can post comments and give feedback to peers about the artwork they created.

(Adapted from a lesson presented by K. Kelly and M. Pasciutti, LITECH Summit 2014.)

STUDENT GOALS

- I can identify an art movement and explain how a historical time period and culture influences artists' work.

- I can write a reflection that critically examines a piece of art and offer my opinion verbally on my own artwork and that of others using general academic vocabulary and art terminology.

- I can publish my work and provide feedback to others in an interactive online community.

ACTIVATE

Distribute QR codes with various artists and movements for students to explore or provide a HyperDoc with links to students working remotely. Each student will select a movement or artist they would like to analyze. Students will then go on a virtual museum tour via the Google Art Project. https://artsandculture.google.com/. Teacher will elicit vocabulary that will help students describe the paintings they are viewing.

CREATE

Create your own artwork reflective of the movement. Take a photo of your artwork, edit the picture, and upload to Artsonia for the exhibit. https://www.artsonia.com/

EVALUATE & ANALYZE

Briefly describe the artist, their culture, and the art movement of that time period. Explain how the movement may have challenged conventional thought at the time.

COLLABORATE & APPLY

In groups, select one art movement to explore. Look at several famous paintings by artists within the art movement that your group has selected to develop some essential understanding about the art movement's key styles. Identify two artists who were famous within the art movement. Select four works that define the key styles of the movement and justify your choices.

DEMONSTRATE

Students visit Artsonia and post feedback on classmates' artwork based on essential understandings of each art movement. Family and community members are invited to visit and post comments.

- What are the key characteristics of the art movement you selected?
- Which aspects of your artwork do you consider successful and why?
- What might you like to improve on in your artwork, and how might you do this?

EXPAND

Students plan a class field trip based on research of local art and cultural institutions.

CONSIDER THIS

OPPORTUNITIES FOR COLLABORATION

Through teacher collaboration, educators gain a more comprehensive understanding of what their students can do independently, what they can do with the right amount and type of support, and what might have to be revisited and retaught in the curriculum. When you and your colleagues work together and examine student work collaboratively, you can reflect critically on both the students' content and language development. Let's take a step further and create an even more collaborative approach to assessment and include ELs themselves in the process. Students can set and periodically review their own learning goals, articulate what they can do independently, and seek support from their peers and teachers as needed. Through this process, they not only gain a stronger sense of agency and ownership of their own learning, but assessment practices become an opportunity for self-advocacy and collaboration.

RESPONDING TO SOCIAL-EMOTIONAL NEEDS—BUILDING RESILIENCE

Educators play a powerful role in setting the emotional tone in the physical or virtual classroom. Through fair, meaningful, and equitable assessment practices, we embrace the values of caring and inclusion. Students must see that they can demonstrate mastery or make reasonable progressions towards achieving it across the core content areas without having full command of the English language. When it comes to assessment, we must also pay special attention to all the pedagogically important emotions (such as motivation, excitement, agency) that positively impact learning outcomes as well as the ones that may hinder learning (fear of failure, embarrassment, and anxiety). By focusing on students' social-emotional needs during assessment practices through affirmations, positive self-talk, and genuine communication, educators provide a sense of security for their students.

CULTURALLY RESPONSIVE-SUSTAINING EDUCATIONAL PRACTICES

Inclusive instructional and assessment practices are one of the hallmarks of culturally responsive-sustaining pedagogy. When educators take a critical stance, they examine implicit bias in the assessment tools and practices they implement and advocate for all students to experience fair, meaningful, and equitable assessments. One recommendation we have based on culturally responsive and sustaining pedagogical beliefs is the use of varied assessment measures including project-based and problem-based learning opportunities, long-term, authentic projects, and multiple ways students can demonstrate their knowledge and understanding of the core content areas and the skills they have developed in the core curriculum and in language and literacy.

RESOURCES OUTSIDE THE SCHOOL CONTEXT

Partnerships with community-based organizations allow for strengthening the school-family-community relationship. Communities reflect the local families and the neighborhoods in which students live. Partnerships within communities may be established with local YMCAs, Boys and Girls Clubs of America, rotary clubs, faith-based associations, or other local neighborhood associations. Consider this: partnerships with community-based organizations will be unique to each community. After-school and summer programs offered by community-based organizations help extend learning opportunities through enrichment classes, clubs, special courses and events, or summer camps. Sports, creative and dramatic arts, music, language, and technology programs are among the many offered after school, during school breaks, and during the summer to keep young people engaged in the community participating in enriching learning experiences.

Which of these ideas resonate with you and could be considered in your context?

☆☆ DIGITAL-AGE EXPLORER'S CORNER

USING DIGITAL PORTFOLIOS FOR ASSESSMENT

JUDY GORIS-MOROFF, HUNTINGTON UFSD

In 2016, Huntington UFSD, with the support of the Superintendent, James Polansky, and the High School principal, Brenden Cusack, offered the newly approved New York State Seal of Biliteracy "NYSSB" program at Huntington High School. The Huntington administration and staff were excited to implement the NYSSB to emphasize the importance of being biliteral, bicultural, and bilingual.

For the student capstone project, Judy Goris-Moroff, Director of World Languages, ENL and Bilingual Programs and her staff proposed essay research papers that would allow students to show command in the target language to the NYSSB committee. The extra work created by the paper discouraged students from participating so the Director and her staff were forced to find a new and more creative way to encourage students to become involved in the NYSSB program.

Ms. Goris-Moroff and the Latin teacher, Ms. Fortunato, brainstormed the idea of having students create and maintain a digital portfolio from 7th grade to senior year in high school, when they would be expected to defend it. The newly created criteria included the tech tools required to create the portfolio and a rubric to assess language proficiency. Teachers quickly recognized the power of digital portfolios and began implementing them in their classrooms. For the first time, students had the opportunity to upload assignments to their Google platform and reflect on their learning. Students became active learners and engaged in the self-evaluation process. They also developed insight into their learning progress and over time, staff members saw a positive change of attitude towards learning a World language and improvement in the target language.

As High School seniors, students are now required to defend their body of work and showcase their growth over the last four years. The digital portfolios provide the learners with a holistic learning and assessment tool to see growth in their language competence and skills in the target language. Huntington educators concluded that the holistic support allowed students to benefit in the enhancement of their emotional growth. The process was efficient in promoting the learners' development at their pace in spite of the learning differences that individual students possess. Since implementing the digital portfolio in 2016, the Huntington School District has dramatically improved student participation in creating and monitoring their digital portfolio as well as proficiency.

Chapter Summary

- A DATELs environment provides fair and equitable assessments that more accurately reflect the academic progress of English learners.

- A DATELs environment provides ELs with authentic learning experiences, digital tools that promote student learning, and multiple ways to show their success in the classroom.

- Authentic assessments that incorporate digital learning resources measure the student's ability to perform a task based on a learning outcome.

- Online behavioral management tools can assess and monitor student behaviors and allow teachers to share information with parents in an online communication platform.

- Blogs and digital portfolios personalize learning and allow students to respond to and reflect on their experiences.

- Digital learning resources provide opportunities to design, develop, and validate new and more effective assessment materials to measure performance that cannot be assessed with conventional testing formats.

PLN Questions

1. In what ways do you measure/assess digital literacy in your classroom?

2. How can authentic assessments that incorporate digital learning resources identify student success in the classroom?

3. How can authentic assessments that incorporate digital learning resources help teachers identify students that need more assistance?

4. Examine traditional and standardized assessments and describe the advantages and disadvantages for ELs.

5. How do authentic assessments that incorporate digital learning resources lower the affective variables that can negatively influence motivation, self-confidence, and anxiety within the classroom for ELs?

6. Give examples of the three perspectives for the assessment of ELs within your classroom: assessment *as* learning, assessment *for* learning, and assessment *of* learning.

CHAPTER 4

Responding and Creating

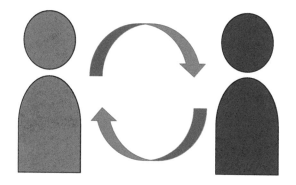

Creativity is intelligence having fun.

(Maxwell, 2003, p. 107)

OVERVIEW

In this chapter we explore the use of digital learning resources to help students express their ideas, develop language and literacy skills, and build creative confidence. Rather than simply enhancing lessons with technology, we need to create instructional routines within a digital learning ecosystem. This structure will support ELs as they engage with peers and express their ideas using multiple modalities. Designing digital content requires planning and research. Students need to synthesize information and communicate content in a way that demonstrates both their academic knowledge and their proficiency in English. Empowering students to create and publish multimedia projects such as videos, podcasts, e-books, and blogs helps them to organize and communicate their ideas more clearly and effectively. The inclusion of images, audio, and video assets accelerates the language learning process by providing a multimodal, multisensory, multimedia experience for the learner. This type of engagement helps ELs to make the shift from being just critical consumers of information to creators of authentic digital media resources. This leap is essential if we want to transform learning experiences for our 21st-century ELs.

 DIGITAL-AGE LEARNING EXPERIENCE

THE SAMR MODEL

Before we can discuss the creation of digital learning ecosystems and the use multimedia content, it is important to become familiar with the SAMR (substitution, augmentation, modification, redefinition) model. The SAMR model facilitates the digital learning transformation and can offer guidance when selecting technology to use with students. When teachers first begin to use technology in their lessons, they often start by substituting what they already do in class with a digital version of the same thing. Flashcards are a good example of this process. Teachers have used paper flashcards for generations. Nowadays, many teachers and students create digital flashcards as a substitution for a traditional instructional practice.

Understanding the SAMR model will help you assess the depth at which technology has been integrated into the curriculum. Dr. Ruben Puentedura (as cited in Boll, 2015) designed this model to guide educators through four levels of technology integration to demonstrate how instructional practices that integrate technology can evolve over time. The first two levels, substitution and augmentation, offer an enhancement to previous practices, whereas the second two levels, modification and redefinition, provide deeper changes that transform traditional practices. Figure 4.1 illustrates how technology can be integrated into instructional tasks with increasing depth.

The four levels according to this model are as follows:

1. *Substitution.* Technology acts as a direct tool substitute with no functional change. For example, if you choose to use flash cards to teach and reinforce vocabulary, now you can have students create flashcards to study vocabulary independently using apps such as Quizlet.

FIGURE 4.1 ● The SAMR Model for Technology Integration

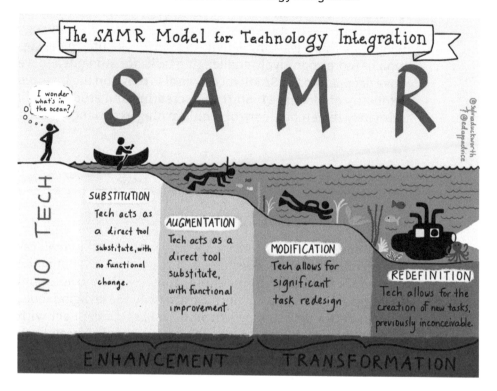

2. *Augmentation.* Technology acts as a direct tool substitute with functional improvement. For example, students create an e-book that incorporates audio and video to practice and learn vocabulary using an app such as Book Creator.

3. *Modification.* Technology allows for significant task redesign. You can reproduce or significantly modify the student task with social networking and collaboration. For example, students collaborate to create rap songs using Flocabulary or publish a blog that includes target vocabulary, video, and links to more information.

4. *Redefinition.* Technology allows for new tasks previously inconceivable. This allows students to interact and engage in learning in ways they could not do in the past and promotes deeper levels of study and research. It provides students with both a choice and personal voice in their learning and is based on problem solving that demonstrates originality of thought and creativity. For example, students from the United States use Teams, Zoom, or Google Meet to video conference with students from Chile who are also learning English. Together they use the target vocabulary in context and collaborate on ways to solve a common problem that affects both communities of learners.

The key to redesigning and redefining classroom tasks in order to reach transformative levels of technology integration is to tap into student creativity. An awareness of the level of technology integration that a learning activity demands will inform the creation of more cognitively challenging tasks for students. As we move deeper into the SAMR model we also move up the inverted taxonomy of Blooms 21. Start with creating and students will ultimately remember more of their learning experiences.

MULTIMEDIA TOOLS FOR ELs

MULTIMEDIA SUPPORT FOR CONTENT

Mobile devices not only enhance instruction and make academic content more accessible for English learners, but when used to their maximum potential, they redefine traditional learning tasks. When students have access to these digital tools, you can better personalize learning for ELs and connect with them and their families, despite the language differences.

MULTIPLE MODALITIES FOR LEARNING

Using digital learning resources for ELs is one way to provide scaffolding to students who are often faced with rigorous content demands while working on acquiring English proficiency at the same time. ELs need alternative pathways to access content.

According to Wilder (2010), the use and creation of multimodal texts will provide students with opportunities to use linguistic, visual, and audio modes in order to experience, conceptualize, analyze, and apply meaning.

Delivering content through tablets or similar mobile devices addresses multiple learning modalities, including visual, tactile, auditory, and kinesthetic learning preferences. It also provides an alternative way for students to demonstrate their content knowledge through the creation of digital media using a wide variety of apps.

APPLICATIONS FOR THE SIX LANGUAGE DOMAINS

The creation of dynamic, interactive reading and writing activities that incorporate video, sounds, links, interactive widgets, and high-quality images redefines viewing and visually representing assignments. ELs can develop active reading skills with the benefit of keyword searches, highlighting, defining, annotating, bookmarking, and researching at their fingertips. Using a text-to-speech feature allows English learners to hear the entire text or vocabulary word or phrase on demand. Tools like Anchor allow ELs to create podcasts that demonstrate content knowledge and speaking skills and can be recorded in multiple languages.

Language domains can be reinforced with the creation of culturally responsive virtual classrooms that include teacher and student avatars or Bitmojis that represent the geographic and linguistic diversity of the students.

Several applications allow students and teachers to create remarkable user-friendly e-books that can be published on the web, printed, shared, or saved and stored locally. These tools offer opportunities for students to visually represent their learning by broadcasting audio and video while developing new language domains. In a survey of AP and National Writing Project teachers, a majority said digital tools encourage students to be more invested in their writing by encouraging personal expression and providing a wider audience for their work. Most teachers also say digital tools make teaching writing easier (Purcell et al., 2013).

EFFECTIVELY COMMUNICATING WITH FAMILIES

The sudden closures of schools in the spring of 2020 made it apparent that innovative changes to the delivery of instruction have to take place in a manner that meets the expectations of progress while also allaying fears of community disruption.

As school districts rethink their education plans, many attempt to strike a balance between public safety, in-person and remote instruction, and effective communication with parents. This new approach places unprecedented focus on technology as the major catalyst driving all aspects of communication and education.

The essential need for technology creates an intrinsic dilemma-is it available and accessible to all education stakeholders? It is important to consider differences through an equity lens to ensure that all students have internet, devices, and technology support. As new technologies are deployed in your school, keep parents informed throughout the implementation process. Students' academic success hinges on parents' understanding and use of classroom technology. While it's important to make sure staff and students are comfortable using technology in the classroom, it's equally beneficial to keep parents engaged, as well.

Schools must also harness the use of technology to effectively communicate with remote learners and families by identifying the most successful ways to deliver important announcements and classroom information. Such technologies may include district websites, emails, blast phone calls, text alerts, and social media sites. As needed, schools should deliver information to parents of ELs in a language or mode of communication that the parent best understands.

Various school districts use over the phone interpreting services such as Propio and Telelanguage. These phone interpreting services provide communication to speakers of more than 200 languages. TalkingPoints, Remind, and WhatsApp allow educators to use cell phones to connect and communicate with families via text messaging directly to their phones in their home language. TalkingPoints provides two-way communication in over 100 home languages.

There are, undoubtedly, many questions parents must consider regarding the education plan for their children:

1. How will expectations of student classwork change for in-person, remote, or hybrid learning?
2. How will school expectations of me as a parent change?
3. What will a typical day in this new classroom environment look like?
4. What is the school's acceptable use policy (AUP)?
5. What training and development resources are being provided to the teachers, students, and parents?
6. What technology do I need to have at home in order for my child to complete assignments?
7. How will schools connect with students and families to support their social-emotional needs?

REMOTE AND HYBRID LEARNING

Remote and hybrid platforms can be challenging for ELs to navigate. When attempting to respond to questions or interact with peers, communication in a video conference may lack many of the nonverbal cues that help convey information and allow us to engage and establish meaningful interactions. In order for ELs to respond and actively engage in a remote learning environment, personal connection must be nurtured and linguistic scaffolds and visual cues must be incorporated. According to Marshall and Kotska (2020), in order to transition instruction from in-person to remote contexts, teachers must consider the four Es: Equity, Enrichment, Engagement, and Empowerment. An emphasis must be placed on creating spaces that facilitate relationship building and create curiosity for learning.

 UNDERSTANDING ELs

COLLABORATIVE PLANNING

One of the best ways to ensure that ELs have access to rich learning opportunities and build academic language skills across the curriculum is to commit to collaborative planning with other teachers of ELs. Teacher collaboration is a critical component of ensuring curriculum continuity and providing instructional consistency. During specially designated co-planning times, general education and ELD/ESL teachers may rely on each other's expertise, share resources, and accomplish the following:

- Establish content and language objectives and instructional procedures for reaching those objectives.

- Determine appropriate modifications and adaptations that will offer the necessary support to ELs if needed.

- Plan differentiated, tiered learning activities that are aligned to ELs' proficiency levels and needs while also challenging them to reach the next level.

- Design formative assessment tools to be used to inform instruction.

- Identify the most appropriate intervention strategies that will respond to the patterns of learning challenges students might face.

- Discuss research-informed best practices and promising strategies they wish to implement.

If ELD/ESL and general-education teachers have the opportunity to co-deliver instruction, each may focus on a different aspect of the lesson and experiment with a variety of co-teaching models while also infusing digital learning resources to enhance content and language attainment (Honigsfeld & Dove, 2019). But keep in mind, you don't need to co-teach to co-plan!

INSTRUCTIONAL DESIGN PRINCIPLES

One of the most important outcomes of the Understanding Language initiative at Stanford University (2013) has been the identification of six principles for designing appropriate instruction for ELs. Although these principles do not explicitly mention multimedia tools, the potential and promise of technology integration is clearly present. Table 4.1 summarizes the six principles and key digital resources that are most closely aligned to each.

LITERACY DEVELOPMENT

Literacy skills are essential for ELs to develop so they can become successful both in and out of school. Among others, August (2018) reports that ELs need explicit instruction similar to that of their English-proficient classmates, including phonemic awareness, phonics, vocabulary, reading aloud,

TABLE 4.1 ● Six Principles for Designing Appropriate Instruction for ELs

PRINCIPLE	RELATED DIGITAL RESOURCES
1. Instruction focuses on providing ELs with opportunities to engage in discipline-specific practices that are designed to build conceptual understanding and language competence in tandem.	Shakespeare in Bits Prodigy Math Game US Geography
2. Instruction leverages ELs' home language(s), cultural assets, and prior knowledge.	Google Translate Remind Talking Points
3. Standards-aligned instruction for ELs is rigorous and grade-level appropriate and provides deliberate and appropriate scaffolds.	Nearpod Jamboard Khan Academy
4. Instruction moves ELs forward by taking into account their English proficiency level(s) and prior schooling experiences.	Newsela Raz-Kids BrainPOP
5. Instruction fosters ELs' autonomy by equipping them with the strategies necessary to comprehend and use language in a variety of academic settings.	EasyBib Notability Evernote
6. Diagnostic tools and formative assessment practices are employed to measure students' content knowledge, academic language competence, and participation in disciplinary practices. (Stanford University, January 2013, p. 1)	Classkick Gimkit Socrative

comprehension, and writing. On the other hand, she suggests that teachers consider additional factors that lead to successful literacy learning such as encouraging peer-to peer interactions and learning opportunities. "Speaking is important to generate feedback, encourage syntactic processing, and challenge students to engage at higher proficiency levels" (para. 24). Academic conversations can even be developed through group emails and text via mobile phone. Group emails and texting facilitate cooperative learning and reinforce language skills. While students interact with each other, they use their languages (both the target language and the home language) functionally. Using a mobile phone to participate in instructional conversations and other learning opportunities can be an essential tool for subgroups of ELs who may have limited access to technology due to a variety of circumstances. One such subgroup is migrant English learners.

Migrant English learners are children whose families typically work in the agricultural industries and as a result, will move from district to district or even from state to state several times within a one- to three-year time frame. Because the families follow the various seasonal crops, migrant ELs are among the most transient student populations. So, the most important strategy is to immediately familiarize them with the instructional routines and include them in class and school activities as much as possible. Enhance the appropriate grade-level or modified curriculum with multiple technology-based scaffolds to make the content accessible and personally engaging and meaningful. Schools and districts should also be mindful of access to devices and bandwidths to ensure digital equity and full participation in learning by all.

It has also been established that during their academic career, students will progress through four major literacy roles as they develop more and more advanced literacy skills (Fang, 2012): ELs, just like their English-speaking peers, must learn how to be code breakers, meaning makers, text users, and text analysts/critics, while also using digital tools in the process.

1. As code breakers, ELs begin by developing foundational literacy skills that provide the basis for decoding text written in English, whether presented in print or digital formats. There are many apps that support developing literacy skills. Bitsboard is one app that can be used to create customized activities to target emerging vocabulary and decoding skills.

2. As meaning makers, ELs begin to make sense of what the text means. First they are most likely to figure out the

literal meaning of any text; however, with appropriate scaffolding and support, ELs can unlock further layers of meaning as well. Platforms such as Actively Learn provide many interactive features that allow students and teachers to annotate and interact with digital text. You can scaffold text by embedding videos and questions that aid comprehension for your ELs.

3. As text users, ELs start to expand their reading skills and tackle a whole variety of texts. They not only comprehend what they read, they also become apt at responding to those texts. When ELs have opportunities to read high-interest texts, as well as make reading choices for themselves, their literacy lives become more authentic. An app that can develop a student's ability to respond to a variety of texts and develop independent reading skills is LightSail. LightSail is an e-reading app that allows for independent and guided reading. Students can make reading choices that are based on Lexile levels. It assesses and tracks a student's literacy development throughout the year and includes social annotation, which is an interactive class discussion component.

4. As text analysts and critics, ELs take the next steps to independence and respond to what they read analytically and critically: they analyze, synthesize, and evaluate the readings while also participating in meaningful discussions with peers and their teachers. With the use of media tools, this type of interaction can reach beyond the classroom. One way to achieve this type of interaction is with online literature circles. Students can lead the circle by selecting a novel and creating their own substantive prompts. ReadWriteThink.org provides many suggestions for implementing online book discussions.

Using multimedia tools to respond and create supports the International Society for Technology in Education Standards for Students ISTE 6. a–d (2017):

6. Creative Communicator

Students communicate clearly and express themselves creatively for a variety of purposes using the platforms, tools, styles, formats, and digital media appropriate to their goals.

MAKE-IT-YOUR-OWN LESSON SEEDS

The following brief overview provides a topic with "seed" ideas that we invite you to "grow" into a full learning experience for your students whether in a remote, hybrid, or in-person classroom setting. The template can also be made into a HyperDoc for students to use.

ADD AND SUBTRACT ZERO GRADES K-2

In this lesson students will be engaged in a Math Flocabulary video that provides students practice with adding and subtracting zero. The video begins with mnemonics to help students remember math facts and contains practice problems which challenge students to sing out the answer. Using Flocabulary allows students to complete math activities by completing vocabulary cards, interacting with a vocab game, reading and responding, and taking a quiz.

STUDENT GOALS

- **I can** create and record my own Math sentences song.
- **I can** identify and analyze vocabulary that describes adding and subtracting zero.
- **I can** view the Flocabulary video and listen to the song. I can sing out the answer before the video.
- **I can** read the Flocabulary Vocab Cards and write the words in a sentence and draw (visually represent) an example of the word.

ACTIVATE
View the Flocabulary Video: Add and Subtract Zero. Choose from the original speed, slower speed, or slowest speed to view the video with the class. Students practice the math problems and sing out the answers before the Flocabulary video does. Then individually students play the Flocabulary Vocab Game and answer questions.

CREATE
Students practice adding and subtracting zero. Then students write their own rhyming sentences using the vocabulary words to create their own rap song.

EVALUATE & ANALYZE

Review the Flocabulary Vocab Cards. Students identify and analyze the vocabulary that describes adding and subtracting zero that are used in their own songs.

COLLABORATE & APPLY

Teacher assists groups of students to create an audio or video recording of their own rap song.

DEMONSTRATE

Students perform their rap songs for an authentic audience (i.e.: parents, other students, community audience) and post audio or video recording on classroom webpage.

REFLECT, ASSESS & REMEMBER

Teacher reads text aloud to students to respond and answer assessment questions. Students complete the online Flocabulary quiz.

EXPAND

Students create their own set of digital flashcards to practice math problems that target their individual learning goals.

CONSIDER THIS

OPPORTUNITIES FOR COLLABORATION

"Multimodality allows all students to use multiple means to engage, interpret, represent, act, and express their ideas in the classroom. For example, as students read, they also might refer to illustrations or diagrams, and as students write, they might also represent their ideas numerically or graphically" (WIDA, 2020, p. 19). Multimodal and multimedia-supported communication also supports collaborative engagements for teachers and students alike, such as collaborative problem solving and inquiry-based or project-based explorations. You might collaborate on creating interdisciplinary learning opportunities and tasks and your students, including ELs of all proficiency levels and language backgrounds may cooperate on multimedia responses to such tasks.

RESPONDING TO SOCIAL-EMOTIONAL NEEDS- BUILDING RESILIENCE

When you encourage student choice in selecting and analyzing resources that will support their learning as well as demonstrating new learning (oral and written text, visual representations, graphic organizers, videos, animation, etc.), they build their autonomy and independence. Project-based learning is uniquely positioned for students to develop such social-emotional competencies and multiliteracies while they "comprehend and compose meaning across diverse, rich, and potentially complex forms of multimodal text, and to do so using a range of different meaning modes" (Victoria State Government, 2018, para. 6).

CULTURALLY RESPONSIVE-SUSTAINING EDUCATIONAL PRACTICES

One hallmark feature of culturally responsive-sustaining pedagogy is having high expectations for all students without defining them by any label or identity marker (including race, gender, ethnicity, linguistic or socioeconomic background). Instruction aligned to high expectations for ELs will incorporate rigorous, content-rich explorations of complex topics using multimodal, multisensory and multilingual resources. Students should see themselves and their lived experiences in the instructional materials and also have an opportunity to critically examine issues related to their lives and communities, including current events and difficult, controversial topics (NYSED, 2019). It is important to keep in mind that rigor never means simply assigning difficult work; instead, when ELs are prepared for rigor, they "understand themselves as contributing members of an academically-rigorous, intellectually-challenging school and classroom community. Students demonstrate an ability to use critical reasoning, take academic risks, and leverage a growth mindset to learn from mistakes" (p. 8).

RESOURCES OUTSIDE THE SCHOOL CONTEXT

To extend and enhance learning for ELs beyond the walls of the classroom or school, you can provide multimodal texts such as picture books, graphic novels, richly illustrated print-based readings as well as multimodal digital resources such as films, video clips, interactive webpages students can access at home. On the other hand, English learners can create multimodal responses to demonstrate understanding through digital media resources. For example, students can collect and organize information and record a video that can be authentically published and shared with a broader audience such as their families via YouTube.

Which of these ideas resonate with you and could be considered in your context?

DIGITAL-AGE EXPLORER'S CORNER

HIDDEN STORIES PODCAST

JAMES HOUSWORTH, ROSEVILLE AREA HIGH SCHOOL

Grade Level: 9–12

When Roseville Area High School teacher James Housworth completed a unit on authentic language products in his teacher training program, he looked for a way to incorporate his years-long interest in podcasts by implementing a segment where students would create their own. He went on to explain that "Not only is a podcast a living, real-world product, but it would also create an opportunity for ELs to produce uninterrupted oral language for 3-5 minutes - in other words, instructional gold."

Mr. Housworth tested out the podcast project with his high school EL Level 4 class. The course typically has a mixture of highly skilled newcomers who are near exiting, as well as LTELs (Long-Term ELs) who might feel stuck in the EL program. This project challenged both groups in different ways, forcing the highly skilled newcomers to develop their fluency and the LTELs to focus and streamline their language.

He learned early on that while podcasts are extremely popular with young adults, they are still making their way into teen culture, so he found it beneficial to begin by having students explore the world of podcasts in class, find the ones they liked, and share recommendations with classmates. Once they discovered K-Pop podcasts, they were hooked!

Once students were ready to begin their podcast project, they interviewed family members and recorded themselves telling their stories. Students then edited and revised their podcast on an iPad app and launched their anonymous classroom podcast called Hidden Voices on Apple Podcasts. Students didn't quite realize what a beautiful thing they had created until they started to see the responses the episodes were getting from listeners within and beyond their own community. Many students, teachers, and even random people online were shocked and touched by the incredible stories that students shared. Many of their personal stories included a mother giving birth while fleeing from war, parents giving up everything to get their son essential medical care, and another narrowly escaping a burning refugee camp.

In short, the podcasting unit was an excellent space for linguistic instruction that included an opportunity for students to interview family members. The 3- to 5-minute podcasts provided the students with many opportunities to craft their vocabulary, grammar, and syntax in this speaking activity. But, equally as important, it allowed the students to share their voices and the voices of their families in a public and authentic way, helping them see that their lives and stories do indeed matter.

Chapter Summary

- The creation of multimedia projects engages all six language domains: listening, speaking, reading, writing, viewing, and visually representing.

- Multimedia projects require ELs to use higher-order thinking skills to shift from consumers to creators of digital content.

- Academic content and language learning are scaffolded by the inclusion of audio, video, and images.

- Multimedia projects provide an alternative way for ELs to demonstrate knowledge.

- The SAMR model can be used to integrate technology to create a digital learning ecosystem that redefines student tasks.

- The creation of multimedia content in cooperative learning settings can help ELs develop literacy skills.

- Schools can leverage technology to effectively communicate with remote learners and families.

PLN Questions

1. How do you design and deliver online learning that builds intrinsic motivation while supporting language learning?

2. How do you move from passive learning to active learning in remote, hybrid, and in-person classrooms environments?

3. Describe the higher-order skills involved when ELs create multimedia projects.

4. How does the creation of multimedia projects support language learning?

5. How do the roles of teachers and students change when the emphasis is placed on digital content creation?

6. How can the SAMR model help you to transform the learning environment for ELs?

7. Describe what technologies are used in your district to communicate with parents in a language or mode of communication that they best understand. In what ways can your district improve communication with families of ELs?

CHAPTER 5

Flipped Learning for ELs

Which activities that do not require my physical presence can be shifted out of the class in order to give more class time to activities that are enhanced by my presence?

(Bergmann & Sams, 2012, p. 96)

OVERVIEW

In this chapter, you will learn about the benefits of using the Flipped Learning instructional model to support students' language and content acquisition and to provide more time for your English learners to interact with their peers in-person or virtually. The Flipped Learning model is an approach that can empower English learners by providing access to subject matter through customized, teacher-created video tutorials. The video tutorial is used to deliver content that would typically be delivered in person by the teacher through a lecture format or in other traditional, direct instruction methods. Whether you are teaching in-person, remotely, or in a hybrid classroom, Flipped Learning invites students to take charge of their own learning by viewing the subject matter asynchronously with the option of stopping the recording, rewinding it, and re-watching it as needed. Then during synchronous instructional sessions, students are better prepared to discuss the topic, ask and answer questions, and problem-solve with their classmates. There are several ways this instructional model benefits English learners. Ultimately, by implementing Flipped Learning methodology for English learners, students will have more opportunity to think critically and to connect authentically with their peers. The most important advantage of this model for ELs is that they acquire core content knowledge and develop active language and literacy practices with ample opportunities for interaction with their peers and teachers.

DIGITAL-AGE LEARNING EXPERIENCE

GETTING READY TO FLIP

As noted by FlippedLearning.org, the model is student centered and emphasizes creativity and collaboration:

> Flipped Learning is a pedagogical approach in which direct instruction moves from the group learning space to the individual learning space, and the resulting group space is transformed into a dynamic, interactive learning environment where the educator guides the students as they apply concepts and engage creatively in subject matter. (https://Flippedlearning.org/definition-of-Flipped-learning/)

Flipping the classroom does require careful preparation. Before starting there are three important questions you can ask yourself:

1. What content and activities do I move to asynchronous class time; what do I put into synchronous class sessions—and why?

2. How do I maximize interaction and differentiation in both asynchronous and synchronous class environments?

3. How do I maximize comprehension and retention for asynchronous work?

In the beginning you must decide if you would like to create your own direct-instruction tutorials or use premade video resources. It's also important to know that there is more than one way to "flip." The model itself is adjustable, and many variations for delivering the Flipped method have emerged as more and more teachers explore this practice in their own classrooms. It is up to you to choose how to best implement flipping for your students.

Some variations include the following:

Flipped project-based learning. Students view a series of videos on a real-world problem and collaborate on a project that seeks a solution.

Flipped mastery. Individualized video tutorials are targeted and informed by data. Students work independently and advance to the next topic only after achieving mastery.

Flipped intervention or enrichment. Video tutorials are created to address the specific remediation needs of the student or to allow the student to expand his or her knowledge of the content.

Flipped peer instruction. Students create video tutorials to assist their peers in learning content. Peers work together to complete classroom assignments.

Marshall (2019) created a Flipped Learning instructional protocol for students to participate in a Flipped Learning experience delivered entirely in a remote learning environment. The *Synchronous Online Flipped Learning Approach* (SOFLA®) includes synchronous, real-time group instruction and collaborative work via a video conferencing platform.

CREATING VIDEOS

If you are new to creating a screencast tutorial, try the following four steps (Marshall & Parris, 2020) that describe the basic components necessary in order to create a video for use in a Flipped Learning environment:

STEP 1: CONTENT

Intentionally select your content for the lesson. Use PowerPoint, Google Slides, or Keynote to create a slide presentation of the information. Since students will be viewing this video before attending class, include information that students will need in order to participate actively in your next synchronous session.

STEP 2: SCREENCASTING

Create a video tutorial by recording your screen while delivering your lecture. Use tools such as QuickTime, Screencastify, Screencast-o-matic, Camtasia, or Loom. Recording your screen offers several opportunities for you to customize the delivery of your content. It is recommended that you keep your webcam on during your presentation so that your students can see you as you present the slides. This has the advantage of providing non-verbal input to your learners. You can also embed captions, or show the movement of your cursor. You can even visit the internet while screencasting and embed demonstration videos in the middle of your presentation. Finally, you can use video-editing tools to modify your screencast.

STEP 3: HOSTING AND SHARING

Upload your presentation video to an online site or service. Your school may have a hosting site, such as Google Classroom or Canvas, your screencasting tool might provide hosting as an option, or you can simply upload the video to your own YouTube channel and choose the "unlisted" designation. Once the uploading is accomplished, you can share the video directly with your students for viewing as a mini-lecture, or you can move to the final step, which includes embedding questions into your video presentation to create an interactive Flipped video lesson.

STEP 4: INTERACTIVE TOOLS

Your fourth step is to turn the video into a lesson in which you ask questions, receive student responses, provide feedback, and gather data on performance. For this step, you can use tools such as Nearpod, Peardeck, PlayPosit, or Edpuzzle. These tools give you options for types of questions to ask, strategically placed in the video. You can also enter feedback for the various responses students may give, at least for the closed-ended questions. With each of these tools you can gather data on your students' responses that will help you to plan your instruction based on their level of understanding and their need for clarification and practice.

Recording screencasts and other types of direct-instruction video tutorials takes time, but doing so allows teachers to scaffold and differentiate the content for the unique language needs of ELs. Whether teachers make their own screencasts or use premade videos for Flipped instruction, teachers and students are ultimately rewarded with more time to explore, interact, and learn.

Some teachers prefer to use video resources from content providers like Discovery Education, Edpuzzle, or Khan Academy, whereas other teachers are flipping "purists" and prefer to create their own videos. There are advantages to both.

Using quality pre-recorded videos can help illustrate concepts in an engaging and effective way and can save time. On the other hand, a lot of time can be lost searching online for the perfect video.

By creating a video of yourself providing the instruction, you can increase the amount of "face" time that you have with students. Making your own video allows you to address various language proficiency levels and home languages. Also, the content can be aligned more precisely to what is happening in your classroom. Over time, you will build your own library of videos to draw from.

QUICK TIPS

There are some basic guidelines when preparing to flip a lesson or a unit of instruction.

VIDEO LENGTH

The length of video should vary according to your students' grade level. It has been suggested that teachers record no more than 1 minute of video instruction per student grade level. In other words, a viewing assignment should not exceed 12 minutes for your high school students. For elementary students, the viewing assignment should not exceed 6 minutes.

SHARING VIDEOS

No matter which method you choose, be sure to inform parents about Flipped instruction and the viewing assignment and share with them how they can help students locate the video online if needed.

After posting the video, give students ample viewing time. Provide scaffolded vocabulary and guiding questions to aid comprehension, as well as graphic organizers for fact collecting. It is better to post several videos at a time to allow students to go ahead or go back according to their needs.

ENGAGING STUDENTS IN THE CLASSROOM

The Flipped Learning Network (https://Flippedlearning.org/) created the four pillars of Flipped Learning. They are: Flexible Learning Environment, Learning Culture, Intentional Content, and Professional Educator. Research conducted by Hung (2017) reveals that the use of Flipped Learning had a positive effect on academic achievement and student attitudes toward learning. Based on these findings, she created an instructional framework using the four pillars of Flipped Learning as they relate to language educators. They are:

- *The F principle of a flexible language learning environment: Provide comprehensible input with flexibility, accommodating individual preferences and proficiency levels, as a means for creating acquisition-rich Flipped classrooms for L2 learners.*

- *The L principle of a language learning culture: Offer interaction opportunities by using active learning strategies to increase learners' L2 exposure and use in the Flipped classroom.*

- *The I principle of intentional linguistic content: Design a mechanism with intentional content focusing on target meanings and forms of L2 to connect the pre-class and in-class activities of the Flipped classroom.*

- *The P principle of a professional language educator: Maintain up-to-date professional knowledge and skills to build a transformative learning community in the Flipped classroom that empowers L2 learners to be active and responsible for their own learning.* (Hung, 2017, p. 188)

Remember that watching a video is only one part of a well-planned Flipped Learning experience. The video is just the beginning of this engaging instructional model. Give careful consideration to the activities you prepare to help your students synthesize and apply the information once they have completed the viewing assignment. Marshall (2019) refers to this process as creating *fertile spaces* by incorporating learning opportunities that are differentiated and hands-on and require students to demonstrate what they have previously learned through their asynchronous viewing.

REMOTE AND HYBRID LEARNING

Using HyperDocs is a great way to promote self-directed learning and to develop student agency for synchronous and asynchronous instruction in remote, hybrid, or even in-person learning environments. According to Clark (2020), author of *The Infused Classroom,*

A HyperDoc is a lesson that is specifically designed to create a student-facing, blended learning experience. Inside of this lesson, students have voice; they are collaborating, creating, communicating and critically thinking their way through the content. It is created to help inspire students' inquiry and curiosity—driving them to exploration, to find answers to their questions, build the background knowledge and support the application of their new knowledge in order to show what they know. Teachers create these lessons with their students in mind, scaffolding every step to help meet their learning needs.

The SOFLA® model provides an eight-step learning cycle that promotes student engagement and fosters the development of an interactive, collaborative community of learners, when teaching in a remote-only learning environment. SOFLA® includes synchronous and asynchronous, structured, multimodal activities that require students to be active learners. The following HyperDoc template (Reproducible 5.1) outlines the Synchronous Online Flipped Learning Approach (SOFLA®) and provides a format for teachers and students to follow during remote learning sessions. Teachers provide directions in the document and embed links to online resources that are needed in order for students to complete their assignment. The HyperDoc is meant to be distributed for students to use.

Table 5.1 provides examples of essential tools for creating a video tutorial for Flipped Learning.

TRACKING STUDENT PROGRESS

Many online platforms track electronically whether a student has viewed the video. Ultimately, a quick check-in at the start of a synchronous class session or a short online survey in an asynchronous module may oftentimes be all the information a teacher needs. Just like any assignment, some students will need to be reminded that the viewing must be completed in order for the student to participate in the other class activities. Student assessment will vary based on the activities designed for each lesson or unit of instruction. Teachers can track student progress using traditional assessments such as tests and quizzes, or they can create rubrics and maintain electronic portfolios to store documents and student-created videos. Nearpod allows teachers to create lessons that track student responses in teacher-led synchronous settings, or students can view and respond in self-paced mode. Flipgrid

STEP 1

PRE-WORK

Pre-work occurs asynchronously. Students view a short video with embedded interactions, complete related readings and/or activities. Insert links here.

STEP 2

SIGN-IN ACTIVITY

The synchronous virtual session begins with an open-ended prompt related to the lesson topic. Students write their responses to the prompt in a shared space and sign their name.

STEP 3

WHOLE GROUP APPLICATION

The entire class collaborates on an activity to clarify misconceptions and/or deepen their learning of the lesson topic in a shared space.

STEP 4

BREAKOUT ACTIVITY

The teacher provides explicit instructions for a structured group activity and directs students to breakout rooms to apply what they have learned. Each group is accountable for a product that documents their work.

STEP 5

SHARE-OUT ACTIVITY

Groups return from breakouts and share their work by presenting their product, information or findings. The other students offer feedback using the SHAC (Share, Help, Ask, Comment) protocol.

STEP 6

PREVIEW-DISCOVERY

The teacher shows the students selected content from the next pre-work and introduces key terms and concepts. Insert links here.

STEP 7

ASSIGNMENT INSTRUCTIONS

The teacher explains each assigned task for the next pre-work viewing assignment, indicating the timeframe and the location of resources. Teacher responds to student requests for clarification.

STEP 8

REFLECTION

The synchronous virtual session ends with an open-ended prompt. In a shared space, students write something that resonated with them from the lesson and sign their name.

 Available for download from **resources.corwin.com/DigitalAgeTeachingforELs**

TABLE 5.1 ● Jump Start Your Flipped Learning: Nuts and Bolts

PRESENTATION TOOLS	SCREENCASTING	HOSTING AND SHARING	INTERACTIVE TOOLS
Keynote	Loom	Canvas	Edpuzzle
Google Slides	Screencastify	Google Classroom	Flipgrid
PowerPoint	QuickTime	YouTube	Playposit

Source: Adapted from Marshall, H.W., & Parris,H. (2020). Jump start your flipped learning: Nuts and bolts. Mosaic. https://sites.google.com/nystesol.org/nystesol-mosaic/

allows students to create and post short video responses in a secure environment and are a wonderful way for ELs to demonstrate both content mastery and language skills. All activities should align to your school's learning standards. In addition, consider the technology standards that your Flipped lesson will address.

> Digital learning environments support the International Society for Technology in Education Standards for Educators ISTE 3.a (2017):
>
> 3. Facilitator
>
> Educators facilitate learning with technology to support student achievement.
>
> Educators:
>
> a. Foster a culture where students take ownership of their learning goals and outcomes in both independent and group settings.
>
> b. Manage the use of technology and student learning strategies in digital platforms, virtual environments, hands-on makerspaces or in the field.

 UNDERSTANDING ELs

FLIPPING THE CLASSROOM FOR ELs

Research is emerging on the positive impact flipping has on learning for ELs, and the anecdotal evidence regarding anticipated outcomes are substantial when considering research-informed and classroom evidence-based practices. Flipped Learning, by definition, requires technology use outside the classroom. Survey your students prior to initiating a Flipped classroom to find out what technology tools are available at home to complete a video or web-based task prior to coming to class. Be prepared to offer alternative ways for ELs to complete the Flipped task if they do not have access to a computer or other device at home, or work on equitable distribution of devices so all students have them. Establish a buddy system or a Flipped Learning after school club if students cannot complete the task alone due to lack of access to technology devices. Explore options including the school library or computer center or the local public library where students may complete their assignment. Videos may also be created for parents, in their home language, so that they can assist their child.

For English learners, the Flipped model has some obvious advantages. While exploring web-based, multimedia resources such as watching a video prior to a synchronous class session (at home, in the school or public library, in an afterschool center or homework club), students can take notes, work at their own pace, pause and rewind the clip, and watch the video as many times as necessary. Watching carefully selected videos naturally lends itself to language learning because the visual content is more readily accessible to students of all proficiency levels than complex textbook syntax and vocabulary.

During synchronous class sessions teachers can spend less time lecturing and have more time to spend engaged with students, giving more personalized instruction. Students apply the information from the video to complete a project or learning task. Teachers become facilitators in this interactive student-centered environment in which ELs have more processing time and more opportunities to develop academic oral and written communication skills. Using class time to complete tasks collaboratively gives ELs more time to synthesize their learning and practice language with their peers.

When English learners regularly interact with their peers, the opportunity to think critically and to use English to connect authentically with others in order to acquire knowledge increases dramatically. Whereas this is perhaps the most important advantage of implementing Flipped Learning for ELs, using multimedia when delivering instruction for ELs also helps them build background knowledge, master vocabulary, infer meaning, and extend their knowledge of a topic.

Although there are many ways to incorporate a Flipped Learning model for ELs, the benefits are similar. Flipping instruction for ELs accomplishes the following:

- Allows for asynchronous instruction while extending learning beyond the confines of the classroom and the school day

- Allows for differentiating instruction through tiered Flipped experiences before and during synchronous class time

- Makes learning visible during synchronous class time as students explore the topic and use language more deeply following the asynchronous learning experience

- Allows more time for immediate teacher feedback on content and language development in class

- Fosters self-motivated, self-directed learning and curiosity in students

ESSENTIAL PEDAGOGICAL COMPONENTS SUPPORTED BY FLIPPED LEARNING

Building on growing classroom-based evidence, we believe that Flipped Learning can contribute to the following critical components of effective instruction for ELs:

1. **Establishing Learning Targets for Content, Language, and Technology**

A learning target is "the lesson-sized chunk of information, skills, and reasoning processes that students will come to know deeply and thoroughly" (Moss & Brookhart, 2012, p. 164). Flipped Learning requires that teachers share the learning target with their students so they understand what concepts and/or skills will be developed as a result of their independent video or web-based learning and the follow-up in-class work. To formulate learning targets as "I can..." statements is highly beneficial for ELs because they have to be able to articulate the outcomes of the learning activity and state the evidence of learning in their own words. The WIDA (2012, 2020) *Can Do Descriptors* could be especially helpful for deciding on reasonable expectations for each grade level cluster and for each language proficiency. The WIDA consortium (see https://wida.wisc.edu/) mission centers around creating quality standards and assessments, conducting research, and offering professional learning opportunities for educators to advance academic language development and academic achievement for linguistically diverse students. More specifically, the Introduction to the most recent WIDA (2020) standards document points out that

Multilingual learners come from a wide range of cultural, linguistic, educational, and socioeconomic backgrounds and have many physical, social, emotional, experiential, and/or cognitive differences. All bring assets, potential, and resources to schools that educators must leverage to increase equity in standards-based systems. Increasing avenues of access, agency, and equity for all multilingual learners—including newcomers, students with interrupted formal schooling (SIFE), long-term English learners (L-TELs), students with disabilities, and gifted and talented English learners—requires educators to be knowledgeable, skillful, imaginative, and compassionate. (p. 18)

WIDA's can-do philosophy indicates a deep belief in the assets and the potential—rather than the deficiencies—of linguistically diverse students. We, too, advocate for such a strength-based approach to working with ELs across all grade levels and content areas.

2. **Activating Students' Prior Knowledge**

Let's agree that all students arrive in school with valuable background knowledge and experience. It has been documented that if "teachers view ELs as bringing valuable knowledge and experiences and see them as eager and capable learners, they are more likely to foster learning environments that engage and challenge ELs" (Hopkins at el., 2019, p. 2298). Additionally, when students have the opportunity to relate their own personal knowledge and experiences to new learning, content attainment is more successful. Further, in his groundbreaking work, Moll (1992) claims that integrating students' *funds of knowledge*—"essential cultural practices and bodies of knowledge and information that households use to survive, to get ahead, or to thrive" (p. 21)—is important in order to offer them a foundation for learning based on prior experiences with their immediate and extended families, their communities, and their culture.

However, when ELs lack or have limited knowledge and experiences related to the core content curriculum, the Flipped experience can help them be better prepared for instruction that directly builds on the Flipped Learning. In a seminal publication, Marzano (2004) also suggested that building background knowledge "should be at the top of any list of interventions intended to enhance student achievement" (p. 4); similarly, Fisher and Frey (2009) expressed urgency when stating that "background knowledge simply has to become an instructional focus if we want to help students make sense of school. We will lose a generation of learners if we don't act now" (p. 20). The importance of assessing, activating, and building background has been recognized by both researchers and practitioners (Honigsfeld, 2019), and we believe Flipping the classroom can substantially contribute to building the much-needed background knowledge for ELs to not only cope with the rigor of the curriculum but to make meaningful personal connections and develop interest in it.

3. **Building Academic Language**

It is now well established in the field of TESOL what Zwiers (2004–2005) observed over a decade ago:

> Academic language is the linguistic glue that holds the tasks, texts, and tests of school together. If students can't use this glue well, their academic work is likely to fall apart. I define *academic language* as the set of words and phrases that (1) describe content-area knowledge and procedures, (2) express complex thinking processes and abstract concepts, and (3) create cohesion and clarity in written and oral discourse. (p. 60)

Classroom interactions are more productive when students come to class having exposure to the key concepts and ideas and understanding key words and phrases that the teacher and their peers are going to use. Beck and colleagues (2013) found that key features of effective vocabulary instruction "are frequent and varied encounters with target words and robust instructional activities that engage students in deep processing" (p. 83). Flipped Learning offers multiple encounters with vocabulary and allows for meaningful engagement with the new content during class time.

MAKING CONTENT ACCESSIBLE

Carefully selected or creatively produced teacher-made screencasts offer a visual window to understanding and allow for personalization of instruction. Through video viewing, complex content becomes more accessible because students can see and hear critical information illustrated on the screen. When selecting premade video, make sure the narrator is clear and easy to understand, or record the videos yourself to ensure the appropriate speed of speech. If closed-captioning is available, in addition to seeing images, diagrams, authentic examples, and other concrete supports for the spoken word, ELs can also follow the script at the bottom of the screen as they watch a video thus receiving yet another channel of input. When ELs have access to a variety of multimodal and multimedia resources that make concepts clear, their comprehension of the target content increases and their receptive language skills expand as well (Echevarria et al., 2016). Digital tools such as Edpuzzle and PlayPosit allow you to embed comprehension questions directly within your own screencast or in premade videos that you find on sites like YouTube or TED-Ed.

ENHANCING STUDENT ENGAGEMENT

Bergmann and Sams (2012) ask one critical question in their book on Flipped Learning: "What is the use of face-to-face time with students?" ELs undoubtedly need opportunities to engage more with the language, explore the content more actively, and interact with all members of the classroom community: English-speaking peer models and fellow ELs as well as teachers, paraprofessionals, instructional aides, and volunteers who might be present in the classroom.

Researchers and practitioners agree that language development takes place in a sociocultural context (Bates, 2019). Holtgraves (2002) observes that "to use language is to perform an action, and it is a meaningful action, with consequences for the speaker, the hearer, and the conversation of which it is part" (p. 5). Varied grouping configurations that allow for both heterogeneous and homogeneous interactions in pairs, triads, small groups, large groups, or teams as well as in whole-class settings lead to more conversations and engaged learning for ELs. By capitalizing on bilingual peer bridges—students who speak the same native language—teachers create opportunities for peer-to-peer support in the shared language, whereas heterogeneous grouping affords more exposure to peer models and clarifications as well as co-construction of meaning with fellow English learners and English-proficient peers.

⌕ MAKE-IT-YOUR-OWN LESSON SEED

The following brief overview provides a topic with "seed" ideas that we invite you to "grow" into a full learning experience for your students whether in a remote, hybrid, or in-person classroom setting. The template can also be made into a HyperDoc for students to use.

WHAT IF? HISTORY PROJECT: THE AMERICAN CIVIL RIGHTS MOVEMENT

GRADES 9-12

The sample lesson we chose for this chapter is an alternate history project, or counterfactual history project.

The counterfactual history project requires students to investigate an event or period in time. Students must do thorough research and then identify a specific moment in history from which to create a point of divergence that ultimately changes the outcome of the event. The point of divergence can be when a student imagines a historical figure making a different decision or it can occur when the circumstances of an event are changed by the student, impacting the historical record. This project offers English learners the opportunity to work collaboratively with their peers to research actual historical events, describe and explain the point of divergence, and create a timeline of these newly imagined events in history.

STUDENT GOALS

- **I can** identify a different point of view in the civil rights movement and explain how individuals and systems create and sustain change.

- **I can** narrate a newly created event in history in the past-perfect tense and use main ideas and supporting evidence in verbal and written format.

- **I can** use primary and secondary sources such as digital, print, and visual materials to research history and create a multimedia presentation.

ACTIVATE

Students watch a video about a significant event that occurred during the civil rights movement (ex: Dr. Martin Luther King's "I Have a Dream Speech," Bloody Sunday, The Freedom Riders). Students view the video as an asynchronous assignment and complete a comprehension activity independently.

CREATE

As a whole class, students create a timeline of the civil rights movement using Padlet and generate key questions about these events and identify specifically a point during the civil rights movement for which to begin your What if? research.

EVALUATE & ANALYZE

Read background information on the history leading up to and immediately following the point in the civil rights movement you are investigating. Research information on the impact that this event had on today's society. Consider what might have happened if the event had never occurred. Complete this sentence: What if…? This is the "point of divergence."

COLLABORATE & APPLY

In groups:

- Identify two events that happened immediately before the point of divergence, and together find two primary-source documents related to those events.

- Between the point of divergence and the present time, introduce two imaginary "new" events to the timeline.

- Describe each of these new events and create your own primary-source documents as evidence of each event. Primary sources can be a journal, newspaper article, speech, photograph, law, bill, court case, cartoon, or other document.

DEMONSTRATE

Create a multimedia representation (video, art installation, slide show, play, song) to present your counterfactual/alternate history. The finished product must include the real and imaginary events, the new primary-source documents you created, and the story of life in America today as a result of the changes you have chosen to make.

REFLECT, ASSESS & REMEMBER

Using a peer review rubric, students critique each presentation and ask the presenters questions for clarification.

EXPAND

Invite a historian from a local college or university to lead a virtual discussion with the students based on their alternate history projects.

CONSIDER THIS

OPPORTUNITIES FOR COLLABORATION

While the first phase of the Flipped Learning experience requires independent/asynchronous work, once students return to the (physical or virtual) synchronous class for further instruction, they may engage in multiple meaningful collaborative tasks to make sense of the material, to engage in disciplinary practices (e.g., read, write, discuss, and conduct experiments like a scientist) and to develop competence across language domains. During these collaborative learning segments, we need to ensure—what Hammond and her colleagues (2018) refer to as—*message abundancy*. Why is it so important? Through an abundance of messaging, we ensure that ELs have multiple meaningful exposures to the same curriculum and language while they engage in independent work, pair work, small group, and whole group instruction.

RESPONDING TO SOCIAL-EMOTIONAL NEEDS-BUILDING RESILIENCE

By inviting students to assess their own learning and engage in independent work through Flipped Learning, teachers help their ELs develop independence, metacognitive awareness, and perseverance. Ritchhart (2015) reminds us that "the chief goal of instruction, right alongside the development of content understanding, is the advancement of thinking" (p. 33). We would argue that the goal of Flipped Learning is to further develop student agency, autonomy, and self-efficacy. As students engage with challenging concepts and rich academic tasks with appropriate scaffolds and supports, they also develop as self-directed and self-motivated learners.

CULTURALLY RESPONSIVE-SUSTAINING EDUCATIONAL PRACTICES

When planning Flipped Learning, remember to leverage students' prior knowledge, interests, and cultural knowledge. Consider using a short self-assessment tool to ensure that your approach is culturally and linguistically responsive and sustaining:

1. How do I increase my knowledge of my students' cultural backgrounds?

2. How do I use knowledge of my students' cultural and familial background to plan instruction?

3. How do I leverage my students' diverse experiences and abilities when planning Flipped Learning?

4. How do I recognize diverse contributions to content areas and social issues?

5. How do I engage my students in discussions that welcome multiple perspectives?

(Adapted from Linan-Thompson et al., 2018, p. 11)

RESOURCES OUTSIDE THE SCHOOL CONTEXT

Recently, Ito et al. (2020) have summarized a decade of research on the gaps between in-school and out-of-school learning. Based on Ito and her colleagues' work, we urge you to consider

(a) how to use the growing number of readily available, free, open-access, online information, learning tools, and resources; (b) how to evaluate the credibility of all this information; (c) how to build upon students' interests and talents; (d) how to capitalize on the power of social media for educational purposes; (e) how to make sense of online learning communities.

Which of these ideas resonate with you and could be considered in your context?

 DIGITAL-AGE EXPLORER'S CORNER

STARTING WITH FLIPPED LEARNING

MARIA ZAMBUTO, 7TH-GRADE PHYSICAL SCIENCE TEACHER, NEW YORK

If you are new to Flipped Learning, you can begin by trying one lesson at a time. Select a lesson you already know well and adapt it to the Flipped Learning model. Maria Zambuto selected a lesson on Circuits that she had previously created and adapted it for remote-only instruction. She decided to try the Synchronous Online Flipped Learning Approach (SOFLA®). She incorporated a variety of interactive digital tools that engaged students in virtual simulations and also hands-on at-home experiments. She provided students with a HyperDoc that led them through each step of the lesson.

7th-Grade Science SOFLA® lesson: Circuits

	PRE-WORK
STEP 1	Students will watch a short and engaging Flocabulary video on Circuits and then complete a few simple follow-up activities that go along with it (vocab game, read & respond, & quiz). Lyric lab will be an optional bonus activity where students can create their own raps/rhymes using the vocabulary words introduced in the video.

	SIGN-IN ACTIVITY
STEP 2	Students: Sign in by sharing on the whiteboard something new learned from the Flocabulary video based on the prompt. (Sample teacher prompts can include: what parts are involved in creating a circuit, what do circuits do, what are some household items use circuits/run on electricity, use a new circuits vocabulary word in your own sentence.)

STEP 3

WHOLE GROUP APPLICATION

Students: Go to the PHET Circuit builder virtual lab simulation on your own device. As I model how to virtually build a simple series circuit, follow along with me and build your own personal circuits using your devices. Manipulate the variables of the circuit such as increasing voltage and adding more light bulbs. (Students will be able to ask clarification questions and will have a chance to practice through this virtual simulation before a real-life experiment takes place.)

STEP 4

BREAKOUT ACTIVITY

Students: You will be placed into cooperative learning groups (team leader, recorder, speaker) to conduct a hands-on lab experiment involving circuits. (Students will be given supplies to build their own simple circuits following the virtual practice: 9V battery, battery clip, alligator clip wires, switch, incandescent lamp.)

Build a simple circuit that can then be used as an insulator/conductor tester. If the lamp illuminates, the material is a conductor, if it does not, the material is an insulator. Make a prediction before each test. Sample materials are: paper, tin foil, waxed paper, penny, toothpick, Lego piece, student-offered items (https://stemrobotics.cs.pdx.edu/node/317).

STEP 5

SHARE-OUT ACTIVITY

Students: Rejoin the whole class as a group. Select a speaker from your group to present the circuit the group decided to build and discuss the group's findings about insulators and conductors in terms of the unique materials their group tested. Other students will offer feedback using the SHAC protocol.

STEP 6

PREVIEW-DISCOVERY

Students: You will be presented with two images of two different types of circuits (series & parallel circuits). Quickly contrast the circuits in your head and think about how they might possibly function in different ways.

STEP 7

ASSIGNMENT INSTRUCTIONS

Watch the teacher screencast hosted in Edpuzzle. Review the circuits and the differences between series and parallel circuits. Answer the multiple choice and open-ended questions that are embedded in the video as you watch and learn the information.

STEP 8

REFLECTION

Students: On the whiteboard, write one thing you learned or found interesting from the lesson (whether it was to do with the Flocabulary video, virtual simulation, or hands-on lab) and sign your name under their comment.

Chapter Summary

- Flipped Learning is a pedagogical approach in which direct instruction moves from the group learning space to the individual learning space.

- Flipped Learning is beneficial to ELs because they can access content to build background through a pre-work viewing assignment.

- The SOFLA® model is a combination of Flipped Learning and remote-only instruction that includes synchronous and asynchronous learning activities

- ELs work collaboratively on inquiry-based learning activities, to clarify information, apply knowledge during class, and practice language with their peers.

- Teachers prepare learning opportunities that are tiered according to language and academic proficiency levels.

- Learning becomes visible for teachers and students during classroom collaboration.

- Teachers guide the process by providing an immediate feedback loop and mini tutorials using the new language and home language as necessary.

PLN Questions

1. What are your objectives when using screencast tutorials and videos with English learners? How would you incorporate these videos in a Flipped Learning environment?

2. When evaluating premade video resources to support your English learners in the content areas, what features are most important to you?

3. What lesson delivery benefits can teacher-made videos and screencast tutorials provide you as an educator? What benefits do teacher-made videos and screencast tutorials provide to ELs?

4. What types of instructional activities can be provided to ELs during the video viewing assignment?

5. After the viewing assignment, how do you support ELs and encourage student interaction during collaborative activities?

6. How can project-based learning and authentic assessments be incorporated into the Flipped Learning environment?

CHAPTER 6

Collaboration and Communication

When teamwork becomes the norm in a school, ELs are better able to exercise their agency, more fully participate in all learning activities, and attain the self-efficacy of independent critical thinkers.

(Cohan et al., 2020, p. xii)

OVERVIEW

In this chapter, we discuss how academic teaming and student "pods" can provide support for ELs by increasing opportunities for collaboration and communication in the target language and how leveraging digital learning resources (DLR) can promote equitable access to instruction and content. According to "Preparing 21st Century Students for a Global Society: An Educator's Guide to the 'Four Cs,'" 21st-century readers and writers need to "build relationships with others to pose and solve problems collaboratively and cross-culturally" as well as "develop proficiency with the tools of technology" (NEA, n.d., p. 16). If we want equitable access to education for our ELs, it is essential for today's English learner to work with others in both in-person and virtual collaborative settings. Collaboration increases opportunities for language development and authentic peer interaction. In addition, collaborating online promotes digital literacy and increases opportunities for you and your colleagues to provide targeted, personalized instruction.

Whenever possible, choose DLR that are "device agnostic" so that students can readily access them from any device. Establish a support system for ELs who might have limited access to technology and scaffold tasks according to their language and technology skills. Be mindful to set up peer tutoring and technology training sessions. In addition, provide parents with appropriate guidance in their preferred language so that they can properly assist students when they are attending school remotely or completing collaborative projects from home. Encourage students to use locally available resources such as community centers and public libraries as needed.

According to Prensky (2010), in a collaborative learning environment, teachers become goal setters, facilitators, and analyzers. His description of "partnering pedagogy" can provide a basis for digital-age EL instruction that incorporates technology to facilitate communication and workflow. In this environment, no matter which learning management system (LMS) is being used, you can encourage students to engage in personalized language learning while interacting with others in online discussions. This includes enabling translation features and read-aloud accessibility options. Essential cloud-based productivity platforms, such as Microsoft Teams and Google Workspace for Education, allow students to brainstorm together and write collaboratively online; however, you need to ensure that ELs are provided additional support in these environments through personalized and group feedback on language as well as content. This can be done by posting written and audio comments and offering suggestions for revision.

Partnering pedagogy in a collaborative environment such as this requires that students become self-directed learners. In this chapter, we discuss the planning and stage setting that must occur in order to create a safe and productive space for students to collaborate and communicate in synchronous and asynchronous learning environments.

 DIGITAL-AGE LEARNING EXPERIENCE

ACADEMIC TEAMING IN THE DIGITAL-AGE CLASSROOM

Academic teaming is a key feature of the 21st-century learning environment. Academic teams are student led groups working collaboratively on authentic learning tasks. It is not cooperative learning, which is defined by teacher led small groups who are all working on the same activity at the same time.

Academic teams should be "small enough to aid in communication and collaboration but also large enough to support diverse opinions, cultural backgrounds, genders, personalities, and skills" (Toth & Sousa, 2019, p. 29). This requires a group of 3–5 students who work together consistently over the school year within establish roles and norms of conduct to complete rigorous tasks together. The use of academic teams enables student voice and choice and develops executive function skills while supporting social, emotional, and cognitive learning for each student. The use of academic protocols and routines such as accountable talk and team roles requires interdependence. For ELs these structures create a supporting environment that increases active participation.

Collaborative learning is not a new concept, but with the digital learning resources now available, you can go even further than before to design collaborative projects that promote language learning and increase communication between ELs and their peers. First, you must ensure that all students have the DLR they need to allow for true student collaboration both synchronously and asynchronously. This requires specific attention to closing the digital divide that leaves many of our linguistically diverse students without equitable access to the appropriate technology or instructional supports necessary to participate in remote and hybrid learning. Strategic in-person, remote, and hybrid learning practices must be identified to ensure that instructional scaffolds are in place and ELs have equal opportunity to actively engage with the content and with their peers.

In order to promote collaboration and communication in the classroom and support ELs as they develop their language skills, there are three design elements to consider:

1. academic teaming/student pods,
2. asynchronous/synchronous learning tasks,
3. curated digital learning resources.

These three elements when combined create your own unique digital-age classroom ecosystem that allows you to promote interactivity and independent learning. We will discuss how to design digital-age learning ecosystems in more depth later in this book. For now, simply consider the following three questions: What does your current digital-age learning ecosystem look like? How does it support academic teaming? How does academic teaming support your ELs?

According to Toth (2019), academic teaming supports equity and access for English learners and is an important instructional design element for the digital-age classroom. If you design student tasks to be completed individually, you may require students to compete rather than share their knowledge with one another. In a digital-age classroom ecosystem we must allow student teams or pods to work together synchronously and asynchronously. Creating student pods and teams allow students to interact with their peers, share information, and learn about the differences and uniqueness their peers bring to the table. Authentic interaction with peers provides expanded opportunities for English language production and develop student agency. Teams and pods also allow teachers to adapt instruction to student needs. "Teaming allows every student to be part of a group, allows every student to have a voice, and allows every student to have opportunity for productive struggle" (Toth, 2019, p. 83).

Also, as we launch ELs into these collaborative learning environments, it is important to support the linguistic diversity of our students so that they can engage effectively with their peers. This requires careful selection of digital learning resources that streamline classroom interaction and enhance productivity. For example, using HyperDocs for student tasks is a simple way to provide tiered instruction in multiple languages while also providing easy access to required online resources.

REMOTE AND HYBRID LEARNING

It is most important that students are given the opportunity to collaborate both synchronously and asynchronously in virtual settings. Your Learning Mangagement System (LMS) is an essential design element for your digital learning ecosystem and will be the hub for productivity. There are several learning management systems (LMS) to choose from. Examples include: Canvas, GSuite for Education, Office365, Schoology, Schoolwork, Seesaw. The learning management system (LMS) is the foundation of your digital classroom environment, but there are many other types of tools to consider as you design a digital classroom ecosystem to support ELs and enhance opportunities for creativity and collaboration. In order for ELs to be successful in remote and hybrid environments, careful attention needs to be given to scaffolding tasks.

Through the scaffolding of tasks for ELs, they can participate more effectively to co-construct meaning, see model texts, use their full linguistic repertoires, and receive teacher and peer feedback on their work. Video conferencing can provide targeted instruction virtually in real time. The strategic use of virtual breakout rooms allows students to work collaboratively with peers of the same or different language proficiency levels. Most video conferencing platforms support live captioning and translation as well as a chat or messaging feature for students to interact with each other and ask questions. The chat feature may reduce the affective filter for ELs and encourage their participation in group discussions. Working with peers on digital whiteboards and mind mapping tools allows ELs to show what they know and visualize their ideas.

 UNDERSTANDING ELs

CREATING A SENSE OF BELONGING

What English learners need is similar to what all students need (August, 2018): a safe, supportive environment in which learning is meaningful and engaging, fear of failure is diminished because risk-taking is encouraged and student-centered learning dominates the instruction. In this context, language is used purposefully, literacy is developed across multiple modalities and students have ample opportunities to work together to make sense of new learning. One significant difference is that ELs have two (or sometimes more) languages to process, figure out, and respond to what is going on in the classroom and beyond. When educators make sure all languages spoken by the students in the classroom are honored as tools of communication through multilingual signs, anchor charts, dictionaries and electronic devices used as resources, and peer bridges (students who speak the same native language interact with each other for peer support and meaning making), students feel welcome and develop a strong sense of belonging. Let's agree to make collaboration the norm in every classroom (Cohan et al., 2020).

Technology offers a wide-open platform for teacher collaboration, as well as collaboration among students. You can also use digital collaboration tools to enhance parent engagement. Use tools such as Google Forms, Remind, and Talking Points to communicate and receive feedback from parents. Keep communication open with families and inform them of school activities and student progress by sharing students' work on your school webpage or classroom blog. Many school districts provide Wi-Fi hotspots to their students for home use and arrange for alternative locations for students to access Internet services when working remotely, such as in community centers and public libraries. Telecommunication companies such as Verizon and Kajeet provide support for these initiatives.

> This instructional model aligns seamlessly with the International Society for Technology in Education Standards for Students 7 a–d (2016).
>
> 7. Global Collaborator
>
> Students use digital tools to broaden their perspectives and enrich their learning by collaborating with others and working effectively in teams locally and globally.

INTERACTION

Vygotsky (1978) is most known for establishing that learning is a process occurring through interaction between people in social, cultural, and historical contexts. Positioning students as thinkers who process and generate new ideas while interacting with others is critical. Over a decade ago, among others, Roskos et al. (2009) established that "children's speaking and listening skills lead the way for their reading and writing skills, and together these language skills are the primary tools of the mind for all future learning" (p. vii). Classroom interaction and collaboration are critical for all learning to take place. Resnick and her team of researchers at the University of Pittsburgh Institute for Learning have developed a set of talk moves known as Accountable Talk. Michaels et al. (2016) defined what makes talk accountable: "For classroom talk to promote learning it must be accountable to the learning community, to accurate and appropriate knowledge, and to rigorous thinking" (pp. 33–34).

What does it mean for ELs? To support cognitive, academic, linguistic, and social-emotional development, ELs need the following:

- Instructional conversations (Goldenberg, 1992; Tharp & Gallimore, 1991) and other academic interaction frameworks that recognize and support ELs as autonomous thinkers who are actively engaged in the learning process along with their teachers and peers.

- Classrooms transformed into a "community of learners" (Tharp & Gallimore, 1991, p. 5) where the verbal traffic is not controlled by the teachers (Cazden, 2001); instead, all learners contribute to discussing and solving authentic problems.

- Conversation protocols that are modeled, explicitly taught, scaffolded, and practiced. For example, Zwiers and Crawford (2009) emphasize the importance of teaching ELs to do the following:
  - Paraphrase and summarize
  - Elaborate and clarify
  - Support one's ideas with details
  - Build on or challenge other students' ideas
  - Apply their ideas to their own lives
- Student-to-student questioning, probing, and the use of evidence in a typical accountable talk interaction (Michaels et al., 2010).
- Universal prompts as suggested by Bambrick-Santoyo and his colleagues (2013). The more ELs hear you apply prompts such as "Tell me more," "What makes you think that?" "Why do you think that is?" and "Why is this important?" to elicit more student talk, the more likely ELs are going to start using and ultimately internalizing these talk moves and prompts with their peers.
- Socratic circles or formal discussions based on a fiction or nonfiction selection in which the leader of the seminar (the teacher or student) asks the group open-ended questions. ELs learn to listen to each other, think deeply and critically, and articulate their own ideas and offer answers in response to what others have contributed.
- Real talk or engagement in genuine student-to-student discussions (Boyd & Galda, 2011). ELs need to learn "how to enter into a conversation; how to take turns without explicit permission from [the teacher]; and how to listen to each other so that they could move from individual contributions without much uptake to talk that was truly conversational, with students responding to one another's comments" (p. 34).
- Intentionally connected talking and learning opportunities. Hammond an her colleagues (2018) aptly state "students [must] have opportunities to talk to learn and to learn to talk (and read and write) academic English" (p. 65).
- Authentic interactions. Most recently, Jeff Zwiers (2020) has advocated for replacing pseudo-communication-heavy lesson activities with authentic communication, which has three key features:
  - purposefully building ideas
  - clarifying and supporting ideas
  - filling information gaps

Technology can facilitate this process with virtual meeting rooms such as Google Meet, Zoom, and Microsoft Teams, where students can communicate face-to-face, in real time, from practically anywhere in the world with Internet access.

FEATURES OF ACCOUNTABLE TALK

Students must be accountable to their learning community by

> listening carefully to others,
>
> adding on to what others have stated,
>
> asking questions and seeking proof,
>
> disagreeing respectfully, and
>
> paraphrasing and summarizing.

Students must be accountable to accurate knowledge by

> using factual information and providing evidence;
>
> using precise, academic language; and
>
> asking others to provide evidence for their claims.

Students must be accountable to rigorous thinking by

> making connections and synthesizing ideas;
>
> making clear statements and providing related evidence;
>
> building justifications, arguments, explanations, and reasons; and
>
> evaluating the claims and arguments of others.

Adapted from the Accountable Talk Sourcebook (Michaels et al., 2010).

COOPERATIVE LEARNING

Cooperative learning has also been widely used in classrooms with English learners as well as with all learners at all grade levels for a considerable length of time. Johnson and Johnson (1999), Slavin (1995), Kagan (n.d.), and others have found cooperative learning to lead to stronger peer motivation, active student engagement, and increased achievement while also providing opportunities for meaningful communication and oral language development. In his early work on visible learning, Hattie (2012) identified peer interactions and peer support as having a positive impact on learning and socializing into the school culture. Hattie specifically suggested the following:

cooperative learning is most powerful after the students have acquired sufficient surface knowledge to then be involved in discussion and learning with peers— usually in some structured manner. It is then most useful for learning concepts, verbal problem-solving, categorizing, spatial problem-solving, retention and memory, and guessing-judging-predicting. (pp. 78–79)

If we want ELs to develop language and literacy skills as well as new understanding in the content areas, we need to offer them ample opportunities for processing information and for using their new language through interaction and collaboration with their peers. To become successful collaborators, they need to work in groups of all sizes: in pairs, in triads, small groups, larger teams, and whole-class discussion.

Varied group configurations and flexible grouping strategies will ensure that ELs learn to cooperate with a range of peers without seeing themselves and others as belonging to static groups. Depending on the goals and objectives of the lesson and the technology tools involved, ELs can work well in both hetero- geneously and homogeneously designed groups. Newly arrived ELs may face multiple challenges as they begin their education in U.S. schools. They need opportunities for simultaneously developing oral language proficiency and essential skills and content to make progress toward grade-level expectations as well as learning about cultural norms and customs in their school, community, and county of residence. Using translation apps such as Google Translate, Tabletop, or Talking Translator can support oral communication.

The use of technology for collaboration plays an important role in helping students take more responsibility for their partici- pation within authentic contexts. Technology also serves as a scaffolding tool so that no matter the proficiency level or what language is spoken in the classroom a student can take initia- tive and contribute to the group task. For example, while read- ing within a platform such as Newsela, the teacher can adjust settings so that the text will match each student's appropriate Lexile level. Long-term ELs who have not made adequate prog- ress in their language acquisition often have strong bilingual oral language skills. They may have even developed native-like fluency in English. Their literacy skills in both the native lan- guage and English are significantly less developed than their oral skills are. A priority for these learners is targeted literacy instruction in both languages, so written communication and collaborative work using digital tools will substantially contrib- ute to accelerating their learning.

MAKE-IT-YOUR-OWN LESSON SEEDS

The following brief overview provides a topic with "seed" ideas that we invite you to "grow" into a full learning experience for your students whether in a remote, hybrid, or in-person classroom setting. The template can also be made into a HyperDoc for students to use.

INSTAGRAM SCIENCE FIELD JOURNAL GRADES 9-12

The Internet has opened the doors for students to conduct authentic, real-world research. Students now have access to institutes of higher education, laboratories, museums, and classrooms around the globe. Understanding how to navigate this essential research tool is a requirement for all learners. However, we must also expose students to real-life scientific discovery and observation through field trips. ELs especially may have limited exposure to the research opportunities surrounding their local community.

According to the National Research Council (NRC) (2012) framework regarding science and engineering practice for planning and carrying out investigations,

> students should have opportunities to plan and carry out several different kinds of investigations during their K–12 years. At all levels, they should engage in investigations that range from those structured by the teacher— in order to expose an issue or question that they would be unlikely to explore on their own (for example, measuring specific properties of materials)—to those that emerge from students' own questions. (p. 61)

In this lesson, students learn how to form their own guiding question for a science field trip, using the Question Formulation Technique (QFT) https://rightquestion.org/what-is-the-qft/ and then collect and post data during the field trip using Instagram. Lastly, students use the data to write a field journal entry.

STUDENT GOALS

- I can collect and share data and conduct research while on a field trip.
- I can write a field journal entry that includes a reflection about what I have discovered as well as questions about what I would like to investigate further.
- I can use Instagram to make observations and share and collect data for my field.

ACTIVATE

Using the Question Formulation Technique students are provided with a question focus (image or text) related to the environment that they will be visiting during their field trip. Each student brainstorms a list of words to describe the image or text.

CREATE

In groups students produce, and then improve as many questions as they can within a given time period https://rightquestion.org/what-is-the-qft/

EVALUATE & ANALYZE

In groups, students prioritize questions and make an action plan for field research. They create a list of possible things to find during the field trip, guided museum tour, or outdoor walking tour.

COLLABORATE & APPLY

Create a public Instagram account for school use. Be sure to get photo release consent. Share your account name and unique hashtag with your teacher. During the field trip find each of the items from the list that your group has created. Take a picture using your cell phone.

DEMONSTRATE

Tag your teacher during the field trip when posting photos. Include a fact you learned or an insightful observation about each particular item from the list. Click the hashtag under any photo and see all the photos your classmates have posted for the field trip.

REFLECT, ASSESS & REMEMBER

Each student writes a field journal entry that summarizes all the data and information collected and what has been learned from the experience. Student entries can be combined with the images from the field trip to create an ebook to share with an authentic audience.

EXPAND

For environmental topics and ideas, visit https://www.epa.gov/students

For games and quizzes, and videos about the environment, visit https://www.epa.gov/students/games-quizzes-and-videos-about-environment

CONSIDER THIS

OPPORTUNITIES FOR COLLABORATION

We must ensure that English learners recognize their classroom as a safe place to engage in disciplinary explorations (math, science, social studies, English language arts, as well as all other specialized curricula) and to develop language, literacy, social-emotional, and collaboration skills across the content areas with peers of all language proficiencies. "When students work together in small groups, they use peer-led dialogic learning to consolidate their thinking" (Fisher et al., 2020, p. 164) as well as challenge each other's thinking to new levels.

RESPONDING TO SOCIAL-EMOTIONAL NEEDS-BUILDING RESILIENCE

Emotions can either help or hinder students' participation in collaborative work. What is our role as educators in setting the tone for a social-emotional climate that is not just conducive to learning but helps ELs thrive? We need to model, guide, and support all students to "show appreciation to others, to build positive relationships, promoting the values of caring and inclusion" (Morcom, 2015, p, 21). One way to achieve that is through student collaboration and thoughtful communication to be infused into every lesson. Through intentional planning and practice that includes social-emotional learning for all, we educators can

- make *lift ups* and not put downs the norm in the classroom
- encourage student communication that is appropriate for the task and social context over grammatical correctness
- explicitly teach students how to build on each other's ideas, acknowledge each other, and accept divergent viewpoints
- show how to use humor and other coping skills
- model how to express empathy and consider others' feelings
- develop students' skills to connect across cultures

As a result, our students engage in learning that not only challenges them cognitively but also supports them socially and emotionally.

CULTURALLY RESPONSIVE-SUSTAINING EDUCATIONAL PRACTICES

In a safe and supportive environment that affirms students' identities and builds on mutual respect, students can learn a range of critical skills, including how to:

- accept each other across differences
- take risks academically, linguistically, and socially

- take responsibility for their own words and actions and hold others accountable for them as well

- express agreements and disagreements and share freely and honestly

An assets-based approach to learning such as the one we just described builds trust within learning communities and plants the seeds for deeper learning (Pijanowski, 2018).

RESOURCES OUTSIDE THE SCHOOL CONTEXT

It has been well established that "collaboration among stakeholders (e.g., district and school leaders, content and language teachers, specialists, support personnel, students, families) is essential for providing multilingual learners high-quality educational experiences that are coordinated and comprehensive" (WIDA, 2020, p. 19). Collaboration and communication do not stop at the doors of a school. Community input that reflects the local context of the school and community engagement that represents authentic parent participation lead to deeper communication and more productive collaboration in and outside the school context.

Which of these ideas resonate with you and could be considered in your context?

 DIGITAL-AGE EXPLORER'S CORNER

VIRTUAL FIELD TRIPS

Mariel Goméz de la Torre-Cerfontaine started virtual field trips on March 16, 2020, when the schools closed in North Carolina due to COVID-19. She started her first contact with a former student who now is a teacher in Peru. Maria also taught in Peru for 15 years before coming to the United States to teach ESL.

During the summer of 2020, her school system opened a virtual school for those students who could not attend face to face. She was very excited to be selected to teach in Summit Virtual Academy. As soon as she started teaching, she noticed most cameras were off, kids didn't want to speak, and in that moment, she knew that she needed to do something different.

Then, she thought about her love of travel. She has visited more than 20 countries and 30 states, and it helped her to grow as a person. Then, she remembered a sentence: "If you can't bring your students to the world, bring the world to your students." So, she started her first trip to Santa Maria, Lima, Peru, where her brother took the class on a virtual visit to the desert and a short walk through the Pacific Ocean. One of the students commented: "Mrs. Mariel, where are the trees?" which made her realize that even though she had showed them pictures of deserts, students did not seem to have grasped the idea of what the desert actually looks like. It was a totally different experience! Of course, we can show students videos of places, but the difference with real virtual trips is that students interact with the guest speaker and their surroundings in real time.

Mariel's focus has been to create situations where students practice authentic academic conversations. These virtual trips spark students' curiosity and a conversation naturally begins between the guest speaker and the students. After the trips, Mariel likes to ask questions to find out what her students have learned. The students are also creating passports with the different countries that they are visiting. They are practicing listening, speaking, reading, viewing, and writing skills in real situations. In one virtual trip to Berlin, Germany students not only visited the city, but also got a chance to see where the Berlin Wall once stood, discuss the fall of the Berlin Wall, and even a bit of the history of World War II. Students were able to compare and contrast life in the United States and Germany before the wall came down. The trips have been so motivating that, on their own, many students started reading books about the various countries that they had been visiting.

Getting closer to December of last year, Maria won a grant to buy books. She told her students that she wanted to buy them a book that her father read to her when she was young. The name of the book is *Around the World in Eighty Days* by Jules Vernes. She invited everyone to come after school to read for 10 minutes. She had 41 students join the book club.

One day, a 4th-grade student who never misses a trip, told her, "Mrs. Mariel, I didn't know that the world was so big." This is so important, how a simple 30- to 40-minute tour can open the eyes of students. After taking virtual trips for four months, two or three times per month, her students are speaking in complete sentences, restating questions, speaking more fluently, and searching for information on their own before and after travelling. They have truly developed a desire for self-guided learning and for continuing to explore the world!

Chapter Summary

- Collaborative learning supports the development of all six language domains for ELs.

- Collaborative learning is beneficial to ELs because it increases opportunities to use the target language to communicate with peers and engage in real-world conversation in order to complete an academic task.

- Students can communicate with authentic audiences and reflect on their work together through virtual communities.

- Teachers can use online learning management systems to communicate and provide a feedback loop for ELs and their families, as they collaboratively track progress, and identify and target the needs of their student.

- Student collaboration can occur remotely in both synchronous and asynchronous settings allowing for access to class assignments and conversations any time.

- Teachers can personalize instruction for ELs by communicating via online posts and group chats.

- Online collaboration tools model and support college and career readiness skills and accelerate learning.

PLN Questions

1. How might academic teaming support your ELs?

2. What unique challenges might ELs face in virtual and in-person collaborative learning environments?

3. When working remotely how can we ensure that ELs have equitable access to digital learning resources in order to complete a collaborative task?

4. Describe your current digital-age learning ecosystem.

5. Which digital learning resources do you find most effective to support workflow, collaboration, and communication?

CHAPTER 7

Virtual Communities and Digital Citizenship

Student efficacy is characterized by students identifying problems to solve or expressive creations they wish to produce. The problems may be related to them personally, the classroom, school, community, state, nation, world, or universe.

(Sulla, 2019, p. 37)

OVERVIEW

One challenge in the digital age that we all must commit to address is to educate students about being responsible digital-age citizens. Learning management platforms such as Canvas, Schoology, and Google Classroom offer a mix of social media and education functions that can be used not only to deliver instruction and provide resources to students but also to create a virtual community of learners. Teacher are also developing creative and meaningful ways to incorporate popular social media sites such as Twitter, Instagram, and Facebook to engage learners and to create networking opportunities that expand learning and sharing beyond the classroom. Yet in order to use these tools successfully, we must also teach digital citizenship.

In this chapter, we discuss the term *digital citizenship* and how we can help students become part of a global digital learning community. Many of our English learners have experienced what it means to be a citizen in one or more countries, but they may not understand what it means to be a digital citizen. We can expand our students' worldview and provide safety for all our students by teaching this very important topic explicitly. Expressions such as "self-reflect before you self-reveal" and "pause before you post" are good starting points for the lessons ELs must learn. In conjunction with this, we can create enriched learning experiences that are inclusive of traditionally marginalized voices and allow students to connect with others throughout the world.

Digital citizenship is a broad term that encompasses many topics related to safe and responsible use of technology and, more specifically, digital communication via the Internet. The ISTE Standards for Students describes good digital citizens as "students who understand human, cultural, and societal issues related to technology and practice legal and ethical behavior" (ISTE, 2016). This includes using technology to actively collaborate with peers to meet learning objectives. For ELs, digital communication means more opportunities to increase authentic interaction through the target language and get additional support while learning new concepts. Even students with limited or interrupted formal education (SLIFEs/SIFEs) who are typically characterized as lacking multiple years of formal schooling in their native countries can, nonetheless, participate in virtual communities and online learning activities. Scaffolding techniques that include visual and hands-on learning opportunities as well as translanguaging (García, 2009, García & Li, 2014) support students with emerging literacy skills. Using bilingual websites such as http://www.colorincolorado.org can provide resources for educators and parents and allow students to draw on their home language to clarify understanding.

There are many helpful organizations that provide online resources that outline the different ways we can engage students in this important conversation. One such organization is The Digital Citizen Institute, which works with school communities around the world to promote positive human connection online. They help communities understand the many different elements of digital citizenship. In *DigCitKids*, it is emphatically recognized that:

> We are in this together. It doesn't matter what language you speak, where you live, or what religion you practice—digital citizenship is all about community and an opportunity to inspire and empower others to take action and become changemakers in their own communities, because once you make an impact locally in your own backyard, it has a ripple effect and continues to influence global and digital communities. (Curran & Curran, 2019, p. 100)

The organization also identifies six "I" statements to consider in order to facilitate positive online interactions and teach students about what it means to be a good digital citizen. Figure 7.1 includes a short description for each of the these six "I" statements.

Incorporating culturally responsive and socially inclusive resources into lessons allows ELs to explore their identity and better understand diversity in their own communities; they also develop intercultural communication and collaboration skills and a heightened awareness of what digital citizenship really means from a global perspective.

FIGURE 7.1 ● "I" Statements for Digital Citizenship in Action

Source: The Digital Citizenship Institute (https://www.digcitinstitute.com/).

⊕ DIGITAL-AGE LEARNING EXPERIENCE

TEACHING DIGITAL CITIZENSHIP

According to Whitby (2014), a connected educator is someone who "embodies a mindset rather than represents someone who does specific things in specific ways" (p. 54). In other words, opening a Zoom, Instagram, Twitter, or Facebook account is the first step, but to truly become a connected educator you must model good digital citizenship and use the Internet to promote positive community engagement, and expand your own knowledge while you teach students how to do the same safely and effectively.

A powerful organization for promoting positive community engagement is Learning for Justice, which was founded by the Southern Poverty Law Center to inform and empower students to work together to be agents of social change and reach beyond the classroom to address issues of equity, identity, and social justice. Their website learningforjustice.org provides free resources to support educators in this mission.

Learning for Justice provides a framework that contains social justice standards divided into four domains: identity, diversity, justice, and action. They also provide lessons and "Do Something!" activities which ask students to demonstrate their anti-bias awareness and civic competency by applying their literacy and social justice knowledge in an authentic real-world context.

REMOTE AND HYBRID LEARNING ENVIRONMENTS

When all students are explicitly taught appropriate online conduct, Internet safety, and how to conduct valid research, they develop a fundamental 21st-century skill set. Common Sense Media (https://www.commonsensemedia.org/educators/curriculum) has published a free digital literacy and citizenship curriculum that offers a scope and sequence for Grades K–12 with lesson plans and teacher guides all available in PDF format and through Nearpod and iBooks. These lessons are aligned with both the Common Core Standards and ISTE Standards and even provide resources in Spanish and French. This curriculum is an easy way to start a dialogue with students about digital citizenship. Topics in this scope and sequence include the following:

- *Student privacy and security.* Strategies for managing online information and keeping it secure (such as creating strong passwords and avoiding scams).

- *Digital footprint and reputation.* How to protect your own privacy and respect others' privacy and reminding students to "self-reflect before they self-reveal" as well as understand the permanence of each and every post.

- *Self-image and identity.* Exploring your online versus offline identity.

- *Creative credit and copyright.* Responsibilities and rights as creators and consumers of online content.

- *Relationships and communication.* Interpersonal and intrapersonal skills related to positive online communication and communities.

- *Information and literacy.* The ability to identify, find, evaluate, and use information effectively.

- *Cyberbullying.* What a student should do if involved in a cyberbullying situation.

- *Internet safety.* Collaborating with others worldwide while staying safe. Distinguishing between inappropriate contact and positive connections.

BUILDING BRIDGES THROUGH GLOBAL PROJECT–BASED LEARNING

Good digital citizenship provides the foundation for ELs to embark on global project-based learning and is a natural extension of their personal experiences from various cultures. PBLworks.org provides extensive resources and research on the use of project-based learning that is standards based and designed to maximize the creative potential of every student. According to PBLworks.org, project-based learning (PBL) "is a teaching method in which students gain knowledge and skills by working for an extended period of time to investigate and respond to a complex question, problem, or challenge." Global PBL involves problem solving for real-world challenges around the globe. In his article "Students Gain Real-Life Insights With Global PBL," Douglas (2015) highlights how facilitating connections with others through global PBL allows students to not only feel the joy that comes through helping others but also better retain what they have learned. He quotes Michael Soskil, a head teacher and curriculum coach, as follows:

> Students are identifying problems in the world and working toward solving them, which is very important, of course, but they are also seeing the good they are doing and want to do more. Kids understand they are learning for a reason, and they connect with this idea for life ... It's neuroscience, in fact, where learning is stored

in long-term memory when a child emotionally connects with the lesson being taught. (Douglas, 2015, p. 27)

You can design projects with ELs that draw on a students' funds of knowledge and experiences such as students' personal journeys from their country of origin, their family histories if they are children of immigrants who were born in the United States, or the cultural richness of their communities. This gives ELs the opportunity to build on their life experiences and culture in order to address real-world issues. It also allows students to transmit their background knowledge to others in the global learning community. To promote global awareness for students and stimulate discussion regarding global concerns, you can also visit the Global Oneness Project (http://www.globalon enessproject.org) for free multimedia resources and lesson plans.

There are several ways you may approach project-based learning but all projects contain certain essential elements. To start you must work together to identify a problem and create a driving question that initiates your search for a solution. Designing projects based on real-world challenges will encourage students to find concrete solutions and become engaged global citizens. Another important element is providing voice and choice. This requires that students be involved in shaping the outcomes and determining the guidelines and agreements for student communication and collaboration throughout the term of the project, as well as respecting the needs of those from other cultures with whom the students may be collaborating. Throughout the process you must facilitate in-depth inquiry, which requires that you work with students to continually develop the context and craft the questions for the project together. All of the work that students engage in should foster the development of mulitliteracies and 21st-century skills. It is one of the end goals and not just a means to an end. Finally, all project-based learning must include a final product that is published to an authentic audience. Using backwards design helps students to identify their end goal and how they will publish and present their completed project before they get started.

TABLE 7.1 ● Project-Based Learning for ELs

PBL ELEMENT	STRATEGIES FOR ELs
Identify a problem/driving question	Capitalize on ELs' funds of knowledge
Find real-world challenge	Promote global awareness and social justice
Provide voice and choice	Allow students to lead project Incorporate culturally responsive and sustaining resources

(Continued)

TABLE 7.1 ● (Continued)

Promote in-depth inquiry	Use sentence frames to generate their own questions about the group investigation
	Provide multilevel and multilingual texts and resources for ELs to choose from in order to research and find answers to their questions
Develop multiliteracies/21st-century skills	Select DLRs that incorporate multimodalities, support and scaffold linguistic demands and content, and promote collaboration
Publish a product to an authentic audience	Include tiered writing tasks for all written products
	Present and publish work in multiple languages
	Align evaluation to include assessment of ELs

This instructional model aligns seamlessly with the International Society for Technology in Education Standards for Students 2 a–d (2016)

2. Digital Citizen

Students recognize the rights, responsibilities and opportunities of living, learning and working in an interconnected digital world, and they act and model in ways that are safe, legal, and ethical.

 UNDERSTANDING ELs

CAPITALIZING ON STUDENTS' FUNDS OF KNOWLEDGE

There has been a strong connection established between culture and language with many researchers suggesting that knowledge is obtained and shared from one's cultural environment (Moll et al., 1992; Moll & Greenberg, 1990). In addition, Esteban-Guitart and Moll (2014) state, "Children are active subjects who create special *funds of knowledge* and *identity* for themselves through their social actions and transactions" (p. 73; italics in original). Many of these social actions and transactions take place outside of school, within the cultural context of the children's home and community lives. We must keep in mind that ELs come to school and to the global learning community with their own funds of knowledge and funds of identity originating from their home experiences. Children learn actively and construct knowledge outside of school as well, thus Moll et al. suggest that educators recognize and use funds of knowledge and identity to assist in student learning in school. We have to see students' "funds of knowledge" as "tool kits" (Esteban-Guitart & Moll, 2014, p. 73) created from the lived experiences students bring and build on in school settings. Suggestions for classroom implementation include the following:

- Inviting students to tell their personal stories (they may use digital tools to do so)

- Making sure students see their lives and experiences reflected in the curriculum as well as the digital resources offered to support the core curriculum

- Nurturing student expertise by publicly recognizing the out-of-school knowledge and skills students have

- Supporting students to make connections between their school and home experiences as they use technology tools

- Making text-to-self, text-to-world, and text-to-text connections (including digital texts) that allow for bridging home and school

Recently, a team at New York University developed a tool they call *Culturally Responsive Curriculum Scorecard* (Bryan-Gooden et al., 2019), the goal of which is to help educators determine if the ELA curriculum is culturally responsive or not. "Curricula that only reflect the lives of dominant populations—for example, White people and culture, nuclear families, or able-bodied people—reinforce ideas that sideline students of color, linguistically diverse students, single parent/multi-generation/LGBTQ+ led families, and students with disabilities" (Bryan-Gooden et al., 2019, p. 4). On the other hand, a culturally responsive curriculum recognizes that diverse groups of people are sources of complex knowledge and experiences, and their perspectives must be valued and fully incorporated in educational materials or curricula. Culturally responsive curriculum also helps students "to connect to experiences beyond their own, examine their own perspective and privilege, and develop a critical consciousness about systems of oppression in order to take action against them" (p. 6).

ELs need to see their lives and lived experiences as well as cultural heritages represented in the curriculum. What we teach and how we teach it cannot be disconnected from the broader cultural aspects of the local community. We must relate new learning directly to ELs' lived experiences so that they can better connect new learning to prior knowledge and also develop the new skills to become college and career ready.

CREATING A SENSE OF BELONGING AND ENGAGEMENT

Over two decades ago, Osterman (2000) found that "students who feel that they belong have more positive attitudes about school, academic engagement and will invest more of themselves in the learning process" (p. 343). English learners, especially some subgroups such as recently arrived immigrant children, refugees, unaccompanied minors, and international adoptees, may find that they no longer belong to their home countries, yet they have not yet been fully accepted and integrated in their new communities. Gay (2000) was among the first to discuss culturally responsive teaching (CRT), which suggests the implementation of a curriculum that allows students to see themselves reflected in it and that the curriculum fosters cross-cultural communication skills among all students. We advocate for all teachers of ELs to develop advanced cultural proficiency skills that support their students' sense of belonging.

When examining factors that have contributed to immigrant students' well-being and academic success, a team of researchers at OECD (2018) found some key indicators that need to be considered: students' sense of belonging at school, their satisfaction with life, their level of school-related anxiety, and their motivation to achieve. There are many more reasons why ELs might be prone to disengage from the learning process, such as not understanding what is being said and taught, limited opportunities for authentic meaning making, limited prior knowledge about certain topics, and limited connections made to their own lives and lived experiences. The challenge we face is to create a learning environment in which ELs become and remain highly motivated and engaged to learn. What motivates ELs is as varied and complex as it might be for any other group of students, yet it is critical that we create a vibrant learning space for them. Peer interaction, project-based learning, visual support, technology integration, choice assignments, and hands-on or kinesthetic learning were reported to be highly motivating for students (Wolpert-Gawron, 2017).

CONTENT AND LANGUAGE INTEGRATION

"Since language development is a complex, long-term process, students should have access to grade-level curriculum concurrently with language instruction" (Gottlieb & Ernst-Slavin, 2014, p. 25). Rigorous culturally and linguistically responsive instruction designed for ELs can no longer focus on language or literacy skills in isolation. The most current understanding about ELs' needs requires that grade-level content and language instruction be integrated: as a result, ELs are taught in a way that they can begin to master the academic content, continue to expand their English language and literacy skills, become fully included members of the school community, and also feel supported in maintaining and enhancing their native language and literacy skills. The combination of these efforts truly leads to fostering global citizenship for all.

Technology has made it possible to conduct interdisciplinary projects within the same school community and beyond. We should harness this opportunity to engage our students in the world around them. An example of this is the EarthEcho Water Challenge https://www.monitorwater.org/ and International Coastal Cleanup Day https://oceanconservancy.org/trash-free-seas/international-coastal-cleanup/.

These projects raise students' awareness and allow them to engage with citizens from around the world in protecting water resources and conducting basic research on the quality of local water samples. The data collected is used to identify trends and relationships across the globe.

MAKE-IT-YOUR-OWN LESSON SEEDS

The following brief overview provides a topic with "seed" ideas that we invite you to "grow" into a full learning experience for your students whether in a remote, hybrid, or in-person classroom setting. The template can also be made into a HyperDoc for students to use.

MYSTERY HANGOUT/SKYPE/ZOOM GRADES 3-8

"Mystery Skype" lessons are interactive and engaging videoconferences. Two classrooms of students connect via Skype, Zoom, or Google Meet without knowing each other's location. Students must ask yes/no questions in order to identify the "mystery" location of the other class. Locations can include classrooms from anywhere in the world. The first class to identify the location of the other class wins. This activity requires an organized team effort, critical thinking, and fact recall, as well as research and map skills. It is a problem-solving activity that provides immediate feedback in an authentic context for ELs to practice listening and speaking.

STUDENT GOALS

- I can think critically to construct, ask, and answer questions to help uncover a mystery classroom's location.

- I can communicate and collaborate effectively with students from various cultures.

- **I can** use Google Maps and other resources to help solve clues about the mystery classroom's location.

ACTIVATE

Using Google Earth, students review the geographic locations that have been previously introduced, and pin locations including names of states, cities, capitals, and counties.

CREATE

Model question format for the Mystery Skype activity. Students prepare a set of 20 questions to ask and 5–10 clues to provide to the other class. Students create a list of "netiquette" rules for participation in online discussion.

EVALUATE & ANALYZE

Assign specific roles to students prior to the call, such as greeters, inquirers, responders, clue trackers, brainstormers, runners, problem-solvers. Rehearse with the class before the actual call.

COLLABORATE & APPLY

During the videoconference try to guess each other's location by asking the prepared questions and developing new ones as needed. Keep track of responses and use your content knowledge, Google Maps, and other classroom resources to solve the mystery.

DEMONSTRATE

The students lead the conversation as the teacher assesses and facilitates the process.

REFLECT, ASSESS & REMEMBER

After the videoconference students reflect on what they learned. Discuss the process, what went well, and what needs to be improved for next time and discuss the product, what new information was discovered about the mystery location and the people they met.

EXPAND

Continue the classroom partnership by collaborating using ePals https://www.epals.com/#/connections or Flipgrid https://info.flipgrid.com/.

Source: DATELs Lesson Seed Hyperdoc Template (Corwin, 2021).

 CONSIDER THIS

OPPORTUNITIES FOR COLLABORATION

Building virtual communities and nurturing digital citizenship is no small feat; as such it must be a joint venture. Educators, administrators, families, and community members may work collaboratively to ensure students are prepared for the ever-changing digital world. As good digital citizens, especially after a once-in-a-century pandemic, our students have to adjust and learn how to support each other virtually, how to be kind and supportive, and collaborate whenever possible.

RESPONDING TO SOCIAL-EMOTIONAL NEEDS-BUILDING RESILIENCE

Digital resilience is a newly emerging concept defined as "the technical, emotional, and critical thinking skills students (and educators) need to enjoy the benefits of the internet while still spotting the dangers and managing the risks" (Snider, 2018, para. 4). All students have to have access to the tools and develop the skills that help them identify potential risks online, keep their information and privacy safe, recognize misinformation, and fight online bullying. To develop digital resilience, students also need to recognize the digital footprint they leave behind and how to appropriately engage with online content.

CULTURALLY RESPONSIVE-SUSTAINING EDUCATIONAL PRACTICES

Culturally responsive-sustaining education does not stop at the classroom door or the school gates. Similar to traditional instructional resources, online materials and digital content must also reflect students' personal and cultural experiences. At the same time, critical engagement with online sources helps students sharpen their skills to distinguish facts from opinions, recognize multiple perspectives, and learn to evaluate the validity and accuracy of information.

RESOURCES OUTSIDE THE SCHOOL CONTEXT

The local community and the students' families must always be considered a rich source of information and shared cultural knowledge. Ishimaru and her colleagues (2016) note how "individuals who serve as *cultural brokers* play critical, though complex, roles bridging between schools and families" (p. 1).

They also emphasize the importance of school leadership to develop a more coordinated effort at building relational trust with the community and to encourage reciprocal cultural brokering. What it means is that families learn about the school culture and norms and expectations and educators learn about the cultural norms and assets of the families. With digital tools and online access, cultural brokering may easily take on a new dimension. During the pandemic, virtual communities also took on a critical role for families to stay connected to the school and support their child's education remotely. A few of these online communities include Facebook pages initiated by parents to stay connected, YouTube Channels launched by teachers to offer virtual announcements or read-alouds, multilingual parent webinars created to inform parents and the community, virtual support groups for families.

Which of these ideas resonate with you and could be considered in your context?

DIGITAL-AGE EXPLORER'S CORNER

LATINOS IN ACTION: THE ELEMENTARY PARTNERSHIP

Hicksville Public Schools has partnered with the Latinos in Action (LIA) Organization to offer ELs in secondary schools an elective course that addresses the student as a whole, tying academics, leadership, and self-development into a single program. Suzy Caceres, a bilingual 3rd-grade teacher from Old Country Road Elementary School, and Omar Garcia, a Spanish teacher at Hicksville High School have taken in-person tutoring and restructured it to a virtual environment as part of the Latinos in Action (LIA) program. The LIA program empowers high school students to be career and college ready through participation in community service in a cross-age tutoring element. LIA high school students serve as role models, mentors, and literacy tutors. The LIA partnership helps the high school and elementary school students develop linguistic proficiency, refine social skills, and deepen their understanding of the value of being bilingual, biliterate, and bicultural.

In order to build relationships with each other, students created an eBook utilizing Google Slides to virtually introduce themselves in an "All About Me" project. The project includes photos, written text, student artwork, images, video, and sound narration to talk about their personal histories and future goals. The presentation described the student, their family, and anything they wanted to share about themselves. The "All About Me" video offers opportunities for emotionally safe (yet still high literacy) communication-based activities for students to share and get to know their tutors and tutees. Students then shared their presentations in the about section of their Google Classroom. The cross-age tutoring element promotes a solid foundation of training, teacher monitoring, and a positive impact on the academic and social lives of all students within the community.

Chapter Summary

- Teaching digital citizenship explicitly is essential to building culturally responsive and sustaining global communities and providing safe and effective online collaboration.

- Incorporating social media into lesson plans expands opportunities for ELs to interact authentically in the target language and get content area support.

- Project-based learning encourages critical thinking and creativity through the use of authentic problem solving.

- Virtual field trips help to bring topics to life and enrich academic background knowledge while helping ELs expand their worldview.

- Global project-based learning allows ELs to tap into their cultural experiences in order to address real-world issues.

- Remote learning environments allow ELs to conduct real-world research, collaborate with other communities of learners, and develop 21st-century skills.

PLN Questions

1. How might you integrate global awareness into cross-curricular lessons that address both language and content development?

2. How can social networking tools be used to engage ELs in issues related to social justice, and authentic, culturally responsive, and sustaining learning?

3. Why is it important to use EL students' funds of knowledge to make new learning relevant and meaningful?

4. How can you engage parents of your ELs to teach digital citizenship when a language barrier or lack of technology skills exists?

5. Describe a project-based learning activity that you have used or would like to use with your students. How would you adapt the activity for ELs?

CHAPTER 8

Fostering a Digital-Age Learning Ecosystem

The crucial task of education is to teach kids how to learn. To lead them to want to learn. To nurture curiosity, to encourage wonder and to instill confidence, so that later on they'll have the tools for finding answers to the many questions we don't yet know how to ask.

(Khan, 2012, p. 155)

OVERVIEW

As we near the end of this book, it is time to explore how to redesign our classrooms. Today's classrooms require digital-age learning ecosystems that promote communication, collaboration, creativity, critical thinking, and culturally responsive and sustaining practices. Within this chapter, you'll discover that creating a digital-age learning ecosystem is not about using every digital learning resource (DLR) available, it's about choosing the right resource for your classroom. DLR should be selected based on their ability to enhance instruction and provide ELs with equitable access to learning. Remember, a digital-age learning ecosystem allows you to differentiate your instruction by creating synchronous and asynchronous learning experiences that support content, language, literacy, and technology targets.

Your classroom's digital-age learning ecosystem exists in both a physical and virtual space. Whether students are working in a shared physical space or within a remote setting, they are each given the opportunity to complete learning tasks independently and within groups. The classroom ecosystem that you design should offer a unique experience for each student that is centered on active learning and engagement with others. ELs must use technology in a productive and collaborative learning environment that will help develop language, literacy, and discipline-specific skills needed for 21st-century careers. When you continue to shift instructional models away from traditional direct instruction practices to student-centered learning, you take on the role of the facilitator. The delivery of instruction is then based on personalized learning, inquiry and research, and student interactions.

As educators, we may not always be able to control whether students have access to technology or Internet resources at home; however, every effort must be made to ensure that English Learners receive equitable access to technology resources. Auxier and Anderson (2020) have found that the need for internet access to complete assignments at home is more pronounced in households with lower incomes and for black and Hispanic students. Ending the digital divide requires collaboration with school leaders, community-based organizations, private industry, and government initiatives. Providing access to the Internet and a full range of digital learning resources in the school building and beyond is vital for ELs.

For English learners, a digital-age learning ecosystem provides opportunities to engage in the curriculum while also gaining essential digital and informational literacy skills needed for real-life situations. Many years ago, November (2012) stated,

> while life outside of our schools has changed dramatically over the past century, we cling to an early industrialized classroom model that often fails to encourage collaboration, innovation, a global work ethic, or critical problem-solving skills. Our students are caught in a process we call "cover the curriculum," regardless of their mastery of the material. (p. 5)

Finally, we have entered a new age of teaching and have shifted away from the previous industrialized model. Now, we must continue to challenge and transform traditional models of instruction that no longer serve the needs of today's and tomorrow's students. Within this chapter, we discuss the components of a digital-age learning ecosystem and digital learning resources (DLRs) as they relate specifically to the instructional needs of English learners.

🌐 DIGITAL-AGE LEARNING ENVIRONMENT

As early as 2007, the Partnership for 21st Century Learning (P21) provided us with a list of discrete skills that students are expected to acquire in order to participate successfully in the fast-paced, globally oriented digital age. Today, this framework has become even more relevant than ever before. Here is a summary of the outcomes described from the P21 framework (2019) and how they relate to ELs today:

1. *Content knowledge and 21st century themes*. In addition to essential core content knowledge in traditional subject areas such as English, world languages, mathematics, science, social studies, music, and art, the framework includes the integration of 21st century themes such as global awareness; environmental, health, and civic literacy; and financial, economic, business, and entrepreneurial literacy. This blend of content knowledge and literacies requires that we provide ELs with a skills base that far exceeds previous academic, cultural, and linguistic demands.

2. *Learning and innovation skills*. These are the skills that separate today's learner from the past and assist them in navigating our complex digital age. The emphasis is on the 4 Cs: creativity, critical thinking, communication, and collaboration. In this book, we add and discuss a fifth "C" for culture. We must raise global awareness, acknowledge diversity and address the need for culturally responsive and sustaining practices in the classroom.

3. *Information, media, and technology skills*. Information and communication technology (ICT) literacy must be integrated into core subject areas and includes a student's ability to create, assess, and apply information and digital media effectively. This also includes understanding and using the most current technology tools. For ELs we must always be mindful of the digital divide that exists between communities of learners and work diligently to pursue equitable access to digital resources for our students.

4. *Life and career skills*. The final student outcome included in the P21 framework recognizes the need to develop a student's social-emotional skills in conjunction with core content knowledge and multiliteracies. Topics included in

this theme include flexibility and adaptation, productivity and accountability, initiative and self-direction, leadership and responsibility, and social and cross-cultural skills. English learners often come to this country with acute social-emotional needs related to the cross-cultural transition they are experiencing and require additional assistance to navigate the life and career skills mentioned.

REMOTE AND HYBRID LEARNING ENVIRONMENTS

Whether you are teaching English in a remote, in-person, or hybrid learning environments, technology is first and foremost an instructional tool and not the subject of instruction. It supports, reinforces, and extends content, language, and literacy learning for English learners. To begin, teachers and administrators must be effective users of digital learning resources. Do you ever find integrating technology overwhelming while you are also working toward meeting the routine demands of meeting learning standards, delivering core content, and assessing your students' progress? As one-to-one mobile learning initiatives have become the norm, you might recognize that creating a digital-age learning ecosystem will support these efforts and encourage a shift in teaching from *what we learn* to *how we learn*.

School leaders can support a culture of sharing and learning for all technology users by modeling the effective use of technology tools. Transitioning to remote and hybrid learning environments and creating a blended model of synchronous and asynchronous instruction requires planning. This includes creating a unified and streamlined digital learning ecosystem throughout the school district, training teachers and support staff to become active learners along with the students, and moving away from lecture-based, direct instruction models to the facilitation of new, student-driven models of instruction. For example, removing language barriers for ELs by incorporating specific multimedia tools used throughout the school district helps English learners share their ideas more freely. Opening the doors to global communication by using social media platforms, videos, podcasts, and blogs allows students to create posts and share learning experiences with others. These learning opportunities provide authentic communication and contextually rich language practice for ELs. The digital-age classroom is a student-centered, culturally responsive, environment with an emphasis on meeting various learning preferences and readiness that encourage ELs to gain understanding in their new language while they may continue to use and develop skills in their home languages as well.

TEACHER ENGAGEMENT

Today's digital learning resources have expanded opportunities to provide real-world experiences by virtualizing your classroom. As we write this book, virtual and augmented reality resources for language learning are developing rapidly and are already a part of the education world. Technology is constantly evolving but finding the technology tools that meet the needs of ELs in your classroom doesn't have to be a daunting task. Whether you are a beginner or an expert in using technology, you can begin to examine ways to integrate technology and design your digital-age learning ecosystem for ELs by:

1. differentiating content and identifying the linguistic demands,

2. identifying how students will demonstrate what they have learned, and

3. redesigning your digital-age learning ecosystem to support diverse learners.

As you create a digital-age ecosystem that meets your needs and the needs of your students, remember, you are not only a "guide on the side," you have become "Chief Opportunity Orchestrator" (COO)—and you are preparing your students for what is now being identified as the 4th Industrial Revolution (Aviles, 2018).

ADVANTAGES FOR ELs

One significant advantage of a digital-age learning environment that supports ELs is an increase in motivation to share learning experiences regardless of a student's language proficiency and prior knowledge. Lowering the affective filter (Krashen, 1988) in this way encourages more participation, which, in turn, can improve academic success. Some key tips:

- Strive to provide a safe school environment where ELs of all proficiency levels can interact with their classmates to improve academic content knowledge and language skills whether in a physical or remote classroom, incorporating communication methods along with technology tools.

- Do not segregate ELs by proficiency level for all learning activities; instead use flexible grouping strategies that allow for different levels of ELs to interact with each other and their English-speaking peers for some of the time, whereas at other times they may be grouped homogeneously, especially when foundational skills are addressed.

- Whenever possible, the students who are proficient and literate in their home languages should have the opportunity to use their native language skills to build comprehension of the target content and to improve communication in their new language as well.

- Build a truly welcoming, inclusive learning community and recognize students' home languages as assets and as cultural and linguistic bridges. Never consider them as something students need to give up and replace with English.

Contrary to the traditional classroom where teachers spent most of their day standing in front of students teaching content, the digital-age learning environment builds on students' interaction in a structured approach, through problem solving, inquiry, and research. You can model and demonstrate learning in virtual and physical classrooms by conducting mini-lessons to build background knowledge, pre-teaching vocabulary, scaffolding instruction, and modeling effective ways to use classroom technology tools. You can address the needs of ELs and provide direct instruction to groups or individuals of all language proficiency levels. The digital learning ecosystem that you design is essential for students while working in groups, pairs, or independently in a learning space that supports flexible grouping and discussion among all learners. When students have a voice in the classroom in this fashion, you enable them to self-direct their own learning process.

THE CLASSROOM SETTING

When planned appropriately, the structure and design of the physical and virtual classroom allows for students to work with peers and encourage investigative learning. The physical design of a traditional classroom provides student learning in a direct-instruction environment, whereas the digital-age learning classroom supports multiple teaching approaches and multiple points of entry to content with access to individualized learning and peer-to-peer engagement. In a digital-age learning classroom, the physical space is set up to allow for movement among students as they actively work within the classrooms in pairs, triads, and other flexible small group configurations and use technology as a tool for learning. Active learning spaces are where "learning happens anywhere and can be synchronous or asynchronous, formal or informal. The change from passive to active learning and the tensions created in this process affect teaching and learning strategies, technologies and space" (Steelcase, 2014, p. 4).

Just as the physical classroom must allow for flexible grouping, movement, and collaboration, the virtual learning space must also be structured to allow for collaboration. What is your role in such scenarios? The first step is to move away from a passive learning environment to an active one. You no longer need to stand in the front of the classroom or conduct a lecture throughout an entire videoconference. Direct instruction must be used with intention to avoid controlling the entire learning process for students. During synchronous class time, you can use technology to collaborate with students and personalize instruction to help groups or individual students through the learning process. You can begin to create a digital-age learning ecosystem by exploring the effects of technology integration on your classroom, including its physical structure or online format. Pause for a moment and reflect on this question: Does your classroom's digital ecosystem support a collaborative and language-enriched environment for ELs?

SELECTING DIGITAL LEARNING RESOURCES

When supporting the unique learning needs of ELs, there are certain features to consider regarding current and emerging technology tools for synchronous and asynchronous learning:

- *Tools that encourage collaboration between the teacher and students.* For example, productivity suites such as Google Workspace and Office 365 streamline the classroom workflow and can support ELs with note taking, word comprehension, and organizational skills that can help drive academic success.

- *Tools that allow teachers to manage lessons, create and share content, and connect with other colleagues (such as learning management systems).* Learning management systems allow you to easily facilitate synchronous and asynchronous learning experiences within their classroom. An LMS allows for class discussions, assignments, and student collaboration within a learning community.

- *Tools that give students options to show off their knowledge (such as screencast tutorials or interactive multimedia presentations).* Multimedia tools allow you to create engaging presentations that include interactive formative assessments. Students can create multimedia presentations by using text, audio, images, and video to tell digital stories and create presentations that demonstrate mastery of content.

- *Tools that develop language skills through listening, speaking, reading, writing, viewing, and visually representing (such as podcasts, blogs, e-books, videos).* ELs can develop language skills by readily accessing digital content to build comprehension and higher-order thinking skills.

- *Tools that allow teachers and students to collect and share information with authentic audiences (for example, QR codes, websites, social media, and parent communication apps).* Classroom information can be quickly accessed and shared remotely with authentic audiences and allow for more interaction among teachers, students, and parents.

Choose digital learning resources that can support academic teaming and provide structure to make collaboration and communication easier for ELs anytime and anywhere there is an Internet connection. Table 8.1 provides a sample of DLRs to consider. For a more extensive list of DLRs, refer to Appendix A.

TABLE 8.1 ● Designing Your Digital-Age Learning Ecosystem

INTERACTIVE PRESENTATIONS	PARENT COMMUNICATION/ TRANSLATION	SOCIAL READING	BRAINSTORMING	MULTIMEDIA	STUDY AIDS
Mentimeter	Class Dojo	Kaizena	Jamboard	Powtoon	Gimkit
Nearpod	Remind	Parlay	Genially	Explain Everything	Kahoot
Peardeck	Talking Points	Perusall	Padlet	Educreations	Quizlet
SeeSaw	Parent Square	Voice Thread	Popplet	Screencast-o-matic	Quizziz

This instructional model aligns seamlessly with the International Society for Technology in Education Standard for Educators 5. c (ISTE, 2017)

Learning Catalyst

5. Designer Educators design authentic, learner-driven activities and environments that recognize and accommodate learner variability.

c. Explore and apply instructional design principles to create innovative digital learning environments that engage and support learning.

 UNDERSTANDING ELs

STUDENT ENGAGEMENT

ELs will acquire language and content only if they have access to the material, if it is presented through a variety of approaches and methodologies with ample support and scaffolding. ELs thrive when we make the lesson comprehensible, meaningful, and cognitively and linguistically engaging. Yet it is not enough for ELs to develop strong receptive skills by listening, reading, and viewing, they need to actively and authentically use multiple modalities to express themselves when speaking, writing, and visually representing ideas.

When selecting a digital learning resource, consider whether it promotes multiple modalities and whether collaboration is possible. One example is Book Creator, which allows students to type text and embed images, video, and audio recordings. Students can use the pen tool for drawing and annotating. They can also collaborate on a book and provide feedback to one another. It can be used with students at any grade level.

When examining what types of engagement leads to deep learning, Ritchhart and Church (2020) point to three specific types of engagement: "(i) engagement with others, (ii) engagement with ideas, and (iii) engagement in action" (p. 8). While Ritchhart and Church might have taken a cognitive focus on learning, the same three approaches may be readily applicable to English language and literacy development:

- When students engage in meaningful exchanges with their teachers and classmates, learning takes place in a social-constructivist context complete with teacher- and peer-support.

- When ELs are given ample opportunities for deep thinking, reflection, and reading, writing, listening, speaking, viewing, and visually representing, as well as using other ways of actively interacting with complex ideas, they develop new conceptual understanding, new learning processes as well as new ways of using language connected to these processes.

- Finally, when new learning is connected to the students' lived experiences and realities, they may want to take action. As learning becomes more personally relevant, language and literacy usage become more authentic, and as a result, students develop their agency.

MEDIATION STRATEGIES

Both researchers and educators agree that content, language, and literacy do not develop in isolation and proficiency in content will only be acquired by ELs if they have access to complex academic materials and opportunities for meaning-making and authentic participation in learning. Mediating language, literacy, and content through a range of approaches is needed for ELs to develop both interpretive and expressive skills. Below we offer six ways to scaffold instruction including offering: Instructional,

Linguistic, Graphic, Visual, Interactive, and Social-Emotional Supports (adapted from Gottlieb, 2018, Honigsfeld & Dove, 2021).

INSTRUCTIONAL SUPPORT

As also suggested by Fisher et al. (2019), instructional support can be successfully offered through the Gradual Release of Responsibility Model (Fisher & Frey, 2008; Pearson & Gallagher, 1983). This framework of instruction starts out with teacher modeling and moves on to delivering instruction to enhance student understanding in small groups and gradually increasing student independence as the lesson progresses. The four steps briefly identified below, however, are not always linear. Based on the cognitive demands of the curriculum and student needs, the four steps may be adjusted and include multiple opportunities for guided instruction or independent work earlier in the sequence.

1. Focus lesson: The teacher sets a purpose for the lesson and models a skill, strategy, or learning task for all learners.

2. Guided instruction: Students practice the new skills alongside the teacher, who differentiates instruction based on students' needs.

3. Student collaboration: Students work in productive learning groups as they engage in a variety of meaningful activities that allows them to interact, solve problems, and gain a clearer understanding of the lesson.

4. Independent practice: Students apply what they have learned.

Classroom instruction that is scaffolded this way allows for various well-supported, structured occasions for students to learn and practice new content and language.

LINGUISTIC SUPPORT

Most frequently, teachers provide linguistic support by addressing students' academic language needs at the word-, sentence-, and discourse-level. For example, you can define key vocabulary, preteach essential words and phrases needed for the lesson, as well as offer the use of sentence frames, sentence starters, or paragraph frames to encourage student participation and enhance language production. Validating students' home language will also offer linguistic support to ELs. Other examples of linguistic supports include when (a) teachers consciously create bilingual peer bridges (two students using both English and their shared home language); (b) when they welcome translanguaging (process in which, "bilingual speakers select meaning-making features [from multiple languages] and freely combine them to potentialize meaning-making, cognitive engagement, creativity, and criticality" (García & Wei, 2014, p. 42), or (c) they adjust their own speech as well as all other text-based or multi-modal resources to be linguistically accessible to all students.

VISUAL SUPPORT

ELs exponentially benefit from seeing what they are also hearing: when visuals are available to supplement verbal input the additional information gained from the images not only aid in comprehension but help frontload the instruction by activating students' prior knowledge or building background knowledge much needed for the forthcoming lesson. You can provide visual support by utilizing models, manipulatives, or realia. Use traditional print images found in photographs, drawings, and magazines; or digital resources that incorporate video clips and images, as well as online learning platforms such as Brainpop ESL or Discovery Education.

GRAPHIC SUPPORT

Similar to the visual support presented above, graphic representations of complex concepts, difficult content, new skills or language input can also contribute to better understanding and easier processing of the lesson. Frequently used graphic supports include a range of graphic organizers, charts, tables, timelines, and outlines. Students can use DLR to create infographics and timelines. Digital mind mapping tools can aid in planning and organizing students' own thoughts as they prepare to speak or write about the new content, thus supporting both oral language expression and written work.

INTERACTIVE SUPPORT

Support may be provided to ELs through a variety of interactive structures. Whole class or large group lessons must be frequently interspersed or supplemented with pair work, triad, or other small group activities. When students *stop and process* or *turn and talk* about the topic, time is allotted for them to formulate their own ideas and practice using academic language. In many classrooms, rotation stations, learning centers, or learning stations are frequently used approaches to groupwork, in which students collaboratively solve a problem, complete a task, and take ownership of new learning and the academic language and literacy skills that are connected to them. Teachers can support ELs when completing station tasks by creating screencast tutorials with clear directions that can be viewed at each station or center.

In addition to all the supports we outlined above, last but not least, we must focus on the affective domain that allows full student participation. We believe that the types of social engagement practices that are established in each classroom will help students learn how to participate in the lessons, how to build meaningful relationships with their classmates and teachers and other members of the school community, and how to develop a sense of belonging. For example, Morcom (2014) reports on collaboratively establishing class agreements that represent various ways to support social-emotional development for all students (see the target skills listed in parentheses):

1. Mutual Respect (interpersonal)

2. Appreciating others (interpersonal)

3. Attentive Listening (communication)

4. Participation/Right to pass (inclusion)

5. Personal Best (positive learning mindset). (p. 21)

When these shared norms and expectations are modeled by teachers and peers and practiced through making explicit connections to students' home lives, background knowledge, and personal experiences, role-playing, daily or weekly class meetings, and more, students learn about themselves and each other, learn how to work in a variety of physical and digital environments, and learn how to use language appropriate for each situation.

TECHNOLOGY READINESS SURVEY

The survey in Table 8.2 can help teachers identify the technology they are currently using and why, their comfort level with using technology, and how that technology is employed in the physical and virtual classroom space. By completing the survey, teacher leaders can recognize professional development needs and assist their peers in planning and creating their own digital ecosystem.

MAKE-IT-YOUR-OWN LESSON SEEDS

The following brief overview provides a topic with "seed" ideas that we invite you to "grow" into a full learning experience for your students whether in a remote, hybrid, or in-person classroom setting. The template can also be made into a HyperDoc for students to use.

TABLE 8.2 ● Technology Readiness Survey

1. Which digital learning resources do you use? Why? In what way do these tools provide instructional support for English Learners?

2. What challenges do you face in designing and managing your digital-age learning ecosystem?

3. What support do you need to effectively integrate digital learning resources into your classroom?

4. How does your physical and virtual classroom support interactive group work?

5. Does the physical and virtual learning space allow you to interact freely with groups?

6. How confident are you when using technology in remote, in-person, and hybrid learning environments?

7. What are the key skills your students will develop while working within your digital-age learning ecosystem?

ADOPT, DON'T SHOP! GRADES 2-4

In this project students learn about animal cruelty and record videos of themselves reading to pets to promote fluency and command of the English language. Students engage and educate community members about the benefits of adopting a pet and the different ways that animals can help people build confidence, increase relaxation, and reduce anxiety.

(This lesson seed was adapted from a lesson created by Jennifer Anderson, Old Mill Road School and Christina Moser, Michael F. Stokes Elementary School)

STUDENT GOALS

- I can write a friendly letter
- I can compare and contrast an animal shelter and a pet store
- I can educate others about animal homelessness, pet care, and pet adoption

ACTIVATE
Students participate in an interactive Nearpod presentation that highlights important information about dog and cat homelessness, overpopulation, and the differences between animal shelters, pet stores, and puppy mills.

CREATE
Students poll their classmates, family members, and friends to find out if they own a pet and how they got their pet. (For example, pet store or adoption center, or other.)

EVALUATE & ANALYZE

Together students interpret the results of the survey and create a graph representing the results.

COLLABORATE & APPLY

Students organize a letter writing campaign and write friendly letters to persuade friends, family, and community members to adopt a pet rather than shop for one. They also describe the many ways in which animals can help people build confidence, increase relaxation, and reduce anxiety.

DEMONSTRATE

Students practice reading fluency and demonstrate how pets can help people to develop confidence and reduce anxiety by creating Flipgrid videos while reading to their own pet or favorite stuffed animal.

REFLECT, ASSESS, & REMEMBER

Students reflect on their experiences to promote change in their community by creating a poster, collage, or drawing based on what they have learned.

EXPAND

Volunteer to participate in local animal shelter or start your own "Reading to Dogs" Program for your community. https://abc7ny.com/reading-to-dogs-bideawee-therapy-kids/5951980/.

CONSIDER THIS

OPPORTUNITIES FOR COLLABORATION

Many teachers collaborate in-person by sharing the same classroom—whether it is through co-teaching or utilizing the same physical space (such as computer labs, library classrooms, and so on). You may also collaborate virtually whether co-teaching in video-conferencing platforms or co-planning in collaborative work spaces online. When you intentionally co-create spaces that offer a welcoming learning environment, you also support students' social emotional needs to develop (a) a sense of ownership and belonging and (b) collaborative skills to be able to work well together. When you create a productive learning environment, you also encourage your students who speak the same language to form bilingual peer bridges and provide multilingual resources for students who have literacy in more than one language.

RESPONDING TO SOCIAL-EMOTIONAL NEEDS-BUILDING RESILIENCE

A crucial aspect of creating a safe place for ELs is ensuring that they can freely express their thoughts, opinions, and feelings using their full linguistic repertoires. Further, students should always be able to make mistakes without shame or embarrassment, take risks academically, socially, and linguistically, and develop a strong sense of agency (sense of self-worth and independence). Some key strategies to create such a learning environment include:

- Create a multilingual space rich with multimodal and multisensory resources

- Ensure that all languages as well as translanguaging is accepted, valued, and embedded in the classroom environment. As García and Wei (2014) note, translanguaging is a process in which "bilingual speakers select meaning-making features [from multiple languages] and freely combine them to potentialize meaning-making, cognitive engagement, creativity, and criticality" (p. 42).

- Make sure respect, care, and empathy are "on display" with sincerity and are a priority for us all.

CULTURALLY RESPONSIVE-SUSTAINING EDUCATIONAL PRACTICES

A core principle of CR-SE is creating a welcoming and affirming learning environment, "where people can find themselves represented and reflected, and where they understand that all people are treated with respect and dignity" (NYSED, 2019, p. 14). Whether you are creating and facilitating a physical, digital, or hybrid learning environment, all your students should experience vibrant, high-quality teacher-to-student and student-to-student interactions and strong, affirming relationships characterized by cooperation, collaboration, and willingness to work together across racial, ethnic, and gender lines.

RESOURCES OUTSIDE THE SCHOOL CONTEXT

Place-based education provides ELs and all their English-proficient peers with a unique opportunity to explore what a particular geographic location may offer: The local environment, that is the community where the students go to school and/or live, may serve as an anchor for the core curricular units in language arts, social studies, math, science, and all other subject matters such as art and music. Exploring the local heritage and history associated with a place where ELs and their families relocated to along with the contemporary cultural landscape may help create a new sense of belonging for students. Place-based learning can easily transfer to the digital landscape and allow students to travel virtually to any place the curriculum is connected. Students can safely view a volcano erupt via a National Geographic video clip or fly over ancient ruins halfway across the world with the help of Google Earth. Virtual field trips open up museums, national parks, and monuments for easy visit; whereas Virtual Reality (VR) pushes the boundaries of place-based learning even further as students are invited to enter imaginary or otherwise unreachable worlds.

Which of these ideas resonate with you and could be considered in your context?

 DIGITAL-AGE EXPLORER'S CORNER

THE "MY NAME, MY IDENTITY CAMPAIGN"

SARA CIOFFI, SHENENDEHOWA CENTRAL
SCHOOL DISTRICT

English learners often encounter teachers who mispronounce their names. As educators, we know that an individual's name is rooted in their identity, language, and culture. Although unintentional, we may not realize that mispronouncing a student's name can have a negative effect on a student's emotional well-being, sense of belonging, and even academic progress. When we mispronounce a name, or downplay the significance of pronouncing names correctly, we are essentially disregarding a student's family and culture (McLaughlin, 2016).

Sara Cioffi, Academic Administrator K–12 ENL/World Languages, addresses this concern in in a profoundly impactful way. She fosters a more culturally responsive-sustaining learning environment for her district by participating in The My Name, My Identity Campaign (https://www.mynamemyidentity.org/). The My Name, My Identity Campaign has two primary objectives. The first one is to raise awareness of the importance of pronouncing names correctly by having members of a learning community sign a pledge to pronounce students' names correctly. The second objective is to post name stories on social media (#mynamemyid) in order to promote caring and culturally responsive-sustaining school environments. The organization provides an online course, campaign tools and resources, and information about equitable instruction. When we show respect for others in this way, we are acknowledging that we are all members of a global community, which is yet another important 21st-century skill.

When Sara launched "The Shenendehowa Name Project" she found meaningful ways to incorporate technology to create a protocol that engaged the entire district in this transformational experience. She began by creating audio recordings of students and/or their parents correctly pronouncing the student's name. She now ensures that every new registrant to the school district has the correct pronunciation of their name recorded when they enroll in school. The sound file is uploaded into their student management system, Infinite Campus. This happens at the registration office so that from the very beginning of the students' journey in a new school, teachers, and support staff can go into Infinite Campus, listen to the sound file, and pronounce students' names correctly.

Chapter Summary

- A digital-age learning ecosystem is based on personalized learning, inquiry, research, and positive student engagement.

- The digital-age learning ecosystem will encourage a shift in teaching from what we learn to how we learn.

- Students use classroom technology tools while working in groups, pairs, or independently in active remote, hybrid, and in-person learning environments.

- Academic teaming allows students to work with peers and encourages investigative learning.

- The digital-age learning ecosystem supports multiple teaching approaches and multiple access points to content to individualize learning and provide peer-to-peer engagement.

- The physical and virtual space is set up to allow for movement among students as they actively work within both environments using technology as a tool to transfer learning.

- Teachers are not restricted to direct instruction models and learning activities flow through synchronous and asynchronous instructional settings.

- Teachers choose digital learning resources that support the instructional needs of ELs.

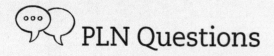 PLN Questions

1. How can a digital-age learning ecosystem be used to meet the needs of English learners?

2. Reflect on a time when you changed your teaching style or lesson to meet the needs of your students. What prompted you to do so? What resources did you change, and what was the result?

3. What steps can you take to move from a teacher-centered environment to a student-centered environment?

4. Does the structure of your physical and virtual classroom encourage collaboration among students?

5. Describe how you can create your own digital-age ecosystem in your classroom in order to support both synchronous and asynchronous instruction.

6. How can other members of your school community help you to create and sustain your digital-age learning ecosystem? (For example: library media specialists, technology integration specialists, content area specialists, building leaders, technology directors, other teachers)

CHAPTER 9

Parting Thoughts

Technology will not replace great teachers but technology in the hands of great teachers can be transformational.

(Couros, 2019, para 5)

IMPLEMENTING CHANGE BY BRIDGING THE DIGITAL DIVIDE

We began Chapter 1 with emphasizing how the digital divide leads to unequal access to technology and information based on socio-economic and cultural factors. We are closing with a call to advocacy to overcome this form of exclusion that directly impacts not only our ELs but our entire education system. For students, inequity impedes not only the overall learning of academic content, but the acquisition of digital literacy skills and opportunities for future employment as well. This discrimination also contributes to a socioeconomic divide among student populations. Before we can truly initiate any change in our classrooms, it is important to provide English learners with equitable access to technology (including devices, Internet access, and all the necessary skills and supports to succeed) within their school communities and in their homes. Limited access to technology is a considerable hurdle that many English Learners must overcome in order to acquire a new language. Finding a solution to bridge the digital divide must involve all education stakeholders: administrators, teachers, parents, students, and community members all have a part to play in accelerating the digital-age revolution in their schools.

The need to address the digital divide and incorporate remote and online learning opportunities has been an ongoing concern for many years. However, the urgency for change has never been more palpable. According to the National Parents Union Coronavirus Impact Study (2020), when asked about educational priorities during the pandemic, 60 percent of parents surveyed indicated that they wanted schools to rethink how students are educated and find innovative ways to move teaching forward. Fifty-four percent identified "providing access to consistent, high-quality remote or online learning for public school" (p. 9) as a top priority. It is clear that bridging the digital divide is essential if we are to prepare our students for life in the digital age. To meet this challenge within each and every one of our school communities, we must first acknowledge that innovative, culturally responsive and sustaining approaches to learning are necessary and that funds must be secured and utilized equitably to ensure that all students and their families can thrive with educational technology.

PROFESSIONAL LEARNING OPPORTUNITIES

How are we doing with professional development in this area? A recent study conducted by the U.S. Department of Education found a statistically significant difference between the percentage of districts that reported they provided professional learning opportunities specifically on the use of digital learning resources (DLRs) to instruct English learners (46%) as compared to those who provided professional learning on the use of DLRs for instructing general education students (79%) (U.S. DOE, 2019, p. 43). In addition, when considering barriers to the use of digital learning resources, the study reported that:

> Eighty percent or more of districts considered students' lack of home access, teachers' need for instructional expertise related to EL-students, teachers technology skills, and lack of knowledge about DLRs for EL students as barriers to some extent or to a large extent. Factors less commonly noted as barriers were insufficient technical

support or troubleshooting hardware or software issues (43 percent) and insufficient network speed and reliability (39 percent). (U.S. DOE, 2019, p. 55)

Studies like this not only capture the current state of the matter but are an urgent call to action! To bridge the digital divide and provide support to all English learners, there needs to be targeted professional development for all teachers, not just ELD/ESL professionals. We must use digital learning resources in order to empower 21st-century English learners to develop multiliteracies in every classroom.

The study by the U.S. DOE also reported that oftentimes, teachers are receiving informal targeted support on various digital tools from their colleagues. This is worth noting because we already know the power of authentic, ongoing teacher collaboration to build professional capacity! Creating professional networking opportunities within school communities that are conducted *for teachers by teachers* has proven to be a useful approach. Our hope is that this book can be a useful tool for joint exploration, discussion, and experimentation with technology in support of ELs. We invite you to expand on the lesson seeds provided and use the PLN questions at the end of each chapter to spark new conversations. Most importantly, working together toward shared goals to create digital equity will help to develop and build trust in the transition process and provide the foundation for lasting change.

CREATING A HIGH-TRUST DIGITAL-AGE ENVIRONMENT

In *The Speed of Trust*, Covey (2008) describes the benefits of building trust to improve an organization's performance. This same philosophy is applicable to educational institutions who strive to create a digital-age environment that is supportive for ELs and for all learners. In a high-trust environment, teachers and students are more likely to experiment with new ideas, take risks, be innovative, and complete tasks more efficiently. When trust is present, most ELs are more likely to participate with enthusiasm in partnered and group activities. Trust is essential for the growth of a culturally responsive and sustaining mindset. Developing trust must include the use of authentic, culturally relevant resources to help students find solutions to real-life problems that require creative, original thinking.

Ultimately, a trusting environment accelerates student growth and helps to develop independent learners. For ELs, who are oftentimes still adjusting to a new cultural environment, and for all students, a sense of safety and trust in the classroom is essential to learning. Furthermore, ELs who feel safe in the classroom will be more likely to tolerate ambiguity and to experiment with the use of English while collaborating with peers, thereby accelerating the language learning process.

We believe that the resources and ideas presented in this book will help you to develop a digital-age learning ecosystem that will improve classroom productivity and promote the development of essential multiliteracy skills for ELs. Your students will become more empowered to work independently and collaboratively and make choices about their own learning journey. As you emphasize the 5 Cs for 21st-century ELs—critical thinking, communication, collaboration, creativity, and culture— they will develop all six language domains—listening, speaking, reading, writing, viewing, and visually representing. As a Chief Opportunity Officer (COO), you will act as a curator of information, and a creator of digital content as you design tasks and projects that set groups of students on an exciting, technology-infused learning journey. This type of student-centered learning dispels the common myth that the use of technology in the classroom creates a culture of isolation. Instead, digital-age teaching for English learners transforms your classroom into a laboratory for learning and authentic exploration. We wish you well on this journey with your colleagues, students, and their families!

 # Appendix A

Technology Tools/Resources

Anchor	Artsonia	Bitsboard	Book Creator	BrainPOP ELL
BuzzSprout	Canva	Class Dojo	EasyBib	Edpuzzle
Edublogs	Educreations	ePals	Epic!Books	Exitticket
Explain Everything	Facebook	FaceTime	FieldTripZoom	Flashcards App
Flipboard	Flipgrid	FlipitPhysics	Flocabulary	Garage Band
Gimkit	Google Arts & Culture	Google Classroom	Google Docs	Google Earth
Google Forms	Google Meet	Google Slides	Google Translate	Google Workspace for Education
iBooksAuthor	iMovie	iStudiez	iTunes	Instagram
iReady	Jamboard	Kahoot!	Kaizena	Keynote
Khan Academy	LightSail	Loom	Mentimeter	Microsoft 365
Microsoft Teams	Miro	Moodle	Nearpod	Newsela
News-o-matic	Notability	OurCongress	OverDrive	Padlet
Parlay	Peardeck	Perusall	PlayPosit	Podbean
Popplet	PowerPoint	Powtoon	Prezi	Puppet Pals
Prodigy Math Game	Propio	QRstuff	QuickTime	Quizlet
Quizizz	Raz-Kids	Read&Write	Remind	Schoology
Schoolwork	Screencastify	Screencast-O-Matic	See.Touch.Learn	Seesaw
Shakespeare in Bits	Skype	S'More	Socrative	Speak It!
Storybird	Symbaloo	Tabletop Translator	Talking Points	TED-Ed
Thinglink	ThinkCERCA	Toontastic	Tumblebooks	Twitter
VoiceThread	Weebly	WeVideo	YouTube	Zoom

online resources ➜ Available for download from **resources.corwin.com/DigitalAgeTeachingforELs**

# Appendix B

ELD/ESL Methodology Resources

Actively Learn: activelylearn.com

Center for Applied Linguistics (CAL): cal.org

Collaboration and Coteaching for ELs: coteachingforells.weebly.com

Colorín Colorado: colorincolorado.org

CommonLit: commonlit.org

Common Sense Media: commonsensemedia.org

Dave's ESL Café: eslcafe.com

Discovery Education Blog: blog.discoveryeducation.com

Digital Citizen Institute: https://www.digcitinstitute.com/

EdSurge: edsurge.com

Educational Resources Information Center (ERIC) on English Language Learners: eric.ed.gov/?q= English+Language+Learners

Edutopia: edutopia.org

ESL at Home: eslathome.edublogs.org

Facing History and Ourselves: facinghistory.org

The Flipped Learning Network: flippedlearning.org

GCF Learn Free: gcflearnfree.org

Global Oneness Project: globalonenessproject.org

International Literacy Association: literacyworldwide.org

ISTE: iste.org

Learning for Justice (formerly Teaching Tolerance): learningforjustice.org

Larry Ferlazzo: larryferlazzo.edublogs.org

Latinos in Action: latinosinaction.org

Mind/Shift: kqed.org/mindshift

My Name, My Identity: mynamemyidentity.org

National Association of Bilingual Education (NABE): nabe.org

National Clearinghouse for English Language Acquisition (NCELA): ncela.ed.gov

New York Times - English Language Learners: nytimes.com/spotlight/learning-lessons-ell

News Literacy Project: newslit.org

Partnership for 21st Century Learning: p21.org

PBL Works: pblworks.org

Project Gutenberg: gutenberg.org

Pronounce Names: pronouncenames.com

Readwritethink: readwritethink.org

Teachers of English to Speakers of Other Languages (TESOL): tesol.org

Teaching Channel: teachingchannel.org

TeachingHistory Digital Classroom: teachinghistory.org/digital-classroom

Teaching Mulitliteracies: https://teachingmultiliteracies.weebly.com/what-are-multiliteracies.html

The Right Question Institute: rightquestion.org

Unite for Literacy: uniteforliteracy.com

Universal Design for Learning: https://udlguidelines.cast.org/

WIDA: wida.wisc.edu/teach/standards

WestEd: wested.org

 Available for download from **resources.corwin.com/DigitalAgeTeachingforELs**

References

Alpert, D., Singer, T. W., & Fenner, D. S. (2020, June 16). From watering down to challenging: Breaking down the wall, one essential shift at a time. *Language Magazine*. https://www.language magazine.com/2020/06/16/from-watering-down-to-challenging-breaking-down-the-wall-one-essential-shift-at-a-time/

Applebee, A. N., Langer, J. A., Nystrand, M., & Gamoran, A. (2003). Student performance in middle and high school English discussion-based approaches to developing understanding: Classroom instruction and student performance in middle and high school English. *American Educational Research Journal, 40*, 685–730. https://doi.org/10.3102/000 28312040003685

Agarwal, P. K. (2019). Retrieval practice & Bloom's taxonomy: Do students need fact knowledge before higher order learning? *Journal of Educational Psychology, 111*(2), 189–209. https://doi.org/10.1037/edu0000282

August, D. (2018). Educating English language learners: A review of the latest research. *American Educator, 42*(3). https://www.aft.org/ae/fall2018/august

Auxier, B., & Anderson, M. (2020, March 16) As schools close due to the coronavirus, some U. S. students face a digital homework gap. *Pew Research Center*. https://www.pewresearch.org/fact-tank/2020/03/16/as-schools-close-due-to-the-coronavirus-some-u-s-students-face-a-digital-homework-gap/

Bambrick-Santoyo, P. A., Settles, A., & Worrell, J. (2013). *Great habits, great readers: A practical guide to K–4 reading in light of the Common Core*. Jossey-Bass.

Bates, B. (2019). *Learning theories simplified*. Sage.

Beck, I. L., McKeown, M. G., & Kucan, L. (2013). *Bringing words to life: Robust vocabulary instruction* (2nd ed.). Guilford.

Bergmann, J., & Sams, A. (2012). *Flip your classroom: Reach every student in every class every day*. ISTE.

Blankstein, A. M. (2007). Terms of engagement: When failure is not an option. In A. M. Blankstein, R. W. Cole, & P. D. Houston (Eds.), *Engaging every learner* (pp. 1–28). Corwin.

Boll, M. (Host). (2015, April 10). Dr. Ruben Puentedura, Creator of SAMR [Audio podcast episode]. In *The Education Vanguard*. https://www.21c-learning.com/podcast/education-vanguard-episode-4-dr-ruben-puentedura-creator-of-samr/

Boyd, M. P., & Galda, L. (2011). *Real talk in elementary classrooms: Effective oral language practice*. Guilford.

Brennan, W. (2013). *School principals and virtual learning: A catalyst to personal and organizational learning*. Unpublished doctoral dissertation, Fordham University, New York. http://www.brennanlearning.com

Bryan-Gooden, J., Hester, M., & People, L. Q.s (2019). *Culturally Responsive Curriculum Scorecard*. Metropolitan Center for Research on Equity and the Transformation of Schools, New York University.

CAST (2020, October 6). *CAST Announces a community-driven process to update UDL guidelines*. https://www.cast.org/news/2020/community-driven-process-update-udl-guidelines

Cazden, C. B. (2001). *Classroom discourse: The language of teaching and learning* (2nd ed.). Heinemann.

Chandra, S., Chang, A., Day, L., Fazlullah, A., Liu, J., McBride, L., Mudalige, T., & Weiss, D. (2020). *Closing the K–12 digital divide* in the age of distance learning. Common Sense Media and Boston Consulting Group.

Ciccarone, A. (2020, February 4). Long Island nonprofit Bideawee helps kids gain confidence by reading to dogs. ABC. https://abc7ny.com/reading-to-dogs-bideawee-therapy-kids/5951980/

Clapper, T. C. (2009). Moving away from teaching and becoming a facilitator of learning. PAILAL, 2(2). http://www.academia.edu/1180001/Moving_away_from_teaching_and_becoming_a_facilitator_of_learning

Clark, H. (2020). The infused classroom: What is a hyperdoc? A quick look. https://www.hollyclark.org/2020/05/03/what-is-a-hyperdoc/

Cohan, A., Honigsfeld, A., & Dove, M. G. (2020). Team up, speak up, fire up! Teamwork to empower English learners. ASCD.

Colorin Colorado. (2018). Addressing student trauma, anxiety, and depression. https://www.colorincolorado.org/immigration/guide/trauma

Couros, G. (2019, June 27). Technology will not replace great teachers but technology in the hands of great teachers can be transformational. https://georgecouros.ca/blog/archives/tag/technology-will-not-replace-great-teachers

Covey, S. (2008). The speed of trust: The one thing that changes everything. Simon & Schuster.

Covili, J. (2012). Going Google: Powerful tools for 21st century learning. Corwin.

Cullen, R., Kullman, J., & Wild, C. (2013). Online collaborative learning on an ESL teacher education programme. ELT Journal, 67(4), 425–434. https://doi.org/10.1093/elt/cct032

Dewey, J. (1944). Democracy and education. The Macmillan Company

Dorfman, L. R., & Cappelli, R. (2017). Mentor texts: Teaching writing through children's literature, K–6. (2nd ed.). Stenhouse.

Douglas, T. (2015, July). Cultural connections: Students gain real-life insights with global PBL. Entrsekt, 24–31.

Dove, M. G., Honigsfeld, A., & Cohan, A. (2014). Beyond core expectations: A schoolwide framework for serving the not-so-common learner. Corwin.

Echevarria, J., Vogt, M. E., & Short, D. (2016). Making content comprehensible for English learners: The SIOP model (5th ed.). Pearson.

Edwards, M. A. (2014). Every child, every day: A digital conversion model for student achievement. Pearson.

Esteban-Guitart, M., & Moll, L. C. (2014). Lived experience, funds of identity and education. Culture & Psychology, 20, 70–81. https://doi.org/10.1177/1354067X13515940

Fang, Z. (2012). Approaches to developing content area literacies: A synthesis and a critique. Journal of Adolescent & Adult Literacy, 56(2), 103–107. https://doi.org/10.1002/JAAL.00110

Fisher, D., & Frey, N. (2008). Better learning through structured teaching: A framework for the gradual release of responsibility. ASCD.

Fisher, D., & Frey, N. (2009). Background knowledge: The missing piece of the comprehension puzzle. Heinemann.

Fisher, D., Frey, N., & Law, N. V. (2020). Comprehension: The skill, will, and thrill of reading. Corwin.

France, P. (2020, April 01). 3 Tips for humanizing digital pedagogy. https://www.edutopia.org/article/3-tips-humanizing-digital-pedagogy

García, O. (2009). Bilingual education in the 21st century: A global perspective. Blackwell/Wiley.

García, O., & Li, W. (2014). Translanguaging: Language, bilingualism, and education. Palgrave Macmillan.

Gay, G. (2000). Culturally responsive teaching: Theory, research, and practice. Teachers College Press.

Goldenberg, C. N. (1992). Instructional conversations and their classroom application (Educational Practice Report 2). National Center for Research on Diversity and Second Language Learning, University of California.

Goldenberg, C. N. (2008). Teaching English language learners: What the research does—and does not—say. American

Educator, 32(2), 8–23, 42–44. http://www
.aft.org/pdfs/americaneducator
/summer2008/goldenberg.pdf.

Gottlieb, M. (2016). *Assessing English language learners: Bridges to educational equity.* Corwin.

Gottlieb, M. (2021). *Classroom assessment in multiple languages: A handbook for teachers.* Corwin.

Gottlieb, M., & Ernst-Slavin, G. (2014). *Academic language in diverse classrooms: Definitions and contexts.* Corwin.

Hammond, J., Cranitch, M., & Black, S. (2018). *Classrooms of possibility: Working with students from refugee backgrounds in mainstream classes.* NSW Government. https://app.education.nsw.gov.au /serap/ResearchRecord/Summary? id=46

Hattie J. (2009). *Visible learning: A synthesis of over 800 meta-analyses relating to achievement.* Routledge.

Hattie, J. (2012). *Visible learning for teachers: Maximizing impact on learning.* Routledge.

Hattie, J., & Yates, G. (2014). *Visible learning and the science of how we learn.* Routledge.

Heritage, M. (2011, Spring). Formative assessment: An enabler of learning. *Better: Evidence-Based Education,* 18–19. http://www.amplify.com/assets /regional/Heritage_FA.pdf

Hobbs, R. (2011). *Digital and media literacy: Connecting culture and classroom.* Corwin.

Holtgraves, T. M. (2002). *Language as social action: Social psychology and language use.* Lawrence Erlbaum.

Honigsfeld, A. (2019). *Growing academic language and literacy: Strategies for English learners.* Heinemann.

Honigsfeld, A., & Dove, M. G. (2010). *Collaboration and co-teaching: Strategies for English learners.* Corwin.

Honigsfeld, A., & Dove, M. G. (2015). *Collaboration and co-teaching: A leader's guide.* Corwin.

Honigsfeld, A., & Dove, M. G. (2022). *Co-planning: Five essential practices to integrate curriculum and instruction for English learners.* Corwin.

Hopkins, M., Gluckman, M., & Vahdani, T. (2019). Emergent change: A network analysis of elementary teachers' learning about English learner instruction. *American Educational Research Journal,* 56(6), 2295–2332. https:// journals.sagepub.com/doi/10.3102/000 2831219840352

Hussar, B., Zhang, J., Hein, S., Wang, K., Roberts, A., Cui, J., Smith, M., Bullock Mann, F., Barmer, A., and Dilig, R. (2020). *The condition of education 2020 (NCES 2020-144).* U.S. Department of Education and National Center for Education Statistics. https://nces.ed.gov/pubsearch/ pubsinfo. asp?pubid=2020144

International Society for Technology in Education Teacher and Student Standards. (2016). http://www.iste.org/standards/ISTE -standards/standards-for-students

Ito, M., Arum, R., Conley, D., Gutiérrez, K., Kirshner, B., Livingstone, S., Michalchik, V., Penuel, W., Peppler, K., Pinkard, N., Rhodes, J., Tekinbaş, K. S., Schor, J., Sefton-Green, J., & Watkins, S. C. (2020). *The Connected Learning Research Network: Reflections on a decade of engaged scholarship.* Connected Learning Alliance.

Johnson, D. W., & Johnson, R. (1999). *Learning together and alone: Cooperative, competitive, and individualistic learning* (5th ed.). Allyn & Bacon.

Kagan, S. (n.d) *Kagan Structures Enhance Student Motivation. Kagan Online Magazine, Issue #59.* https://www.kaganonline.com /free_articles/dr_spencer_kagan/492 /Kagan-Structures-Enhance-Student -Motivation

Khan, S. (2012). *The one world schoolhouse education reimagined.* Twelve.

Krashen, S. D. (1988). *Second language acquisition and second language learning.* Prentice-Hall International.

Krashen, S. (2014). *Stephen Krashen's theory of second language acquisition.* http://sk .com.br/sk-krash.html

Lesaux, N. K., Phillips Galloway, E., & Marietta, S. H. (2016) *Teaching advanced literacy skills: A guide for leaders in linguistically diverse dchools.* The Guilford Press.

Lenski, S. D., Ehlers-Zavala, F., Daniel, M., & Sun-Irminger, X. (2006). Assessing English-language learners in mainstream classrooms. *The Reading Teacher, 60*(1), 24–34.

Linan-Thompson, S., Lara-Martinez, J. A., & Cavazos, L. O. (2018). Exploring the intersection of evidence-based practices and culturally and linguistically responsive practices. *Intervention in School and Clinic, 54*(1), 6-13. https://doi.org/10.1177/1053451218762574

Linton, C. (2011). *Equity 101: The equity framework.* Corwin.

Lundy-Ponce, G. (2010). *Migrant students: What we need to know to help them succeed.* http://www.colorincolorado.org/article/migrant-students-what-we-need-know-help-them-succeed

Marshall, H. W. (2019, April 1). 6 models of flipped Learning instruction. *TESOL Connections.* http://newsmanager.commpartners.com/tesolc/issues/2019-04-01/2.html

Marshall, H. W., & DeCapua, A. (2013). *Making the transition to classroom success: Culturally responsive teaching for struggling language learners.* University of Michigan Press.

Marshall, H. W., & Kotska, I. (2020, August) Fostering teaching presence through the synchronous online flipped learning approach. *TESL-EJ, 24*(2), 1-14. https://www.tesl-ej.org/wordpress/issues/volume24/ej94/ej94int/

Marshall, H. W., & Parris, H. (2020). Jump start your flipped learning: Nuts and bolts. *Mosaic.* https://sites.google.com/nystesol.org/nys-tesol-mosaic/

Marzano, R. J. (2004). *Building background knowledge for academic achievement: Research on what works in schools.* ASCD.

Maxwell, J. C. (2003). *Thinking for a change: 11 ways highly successful people approach life and work.* Warner Books.

McLaughlin, C. (2016, September 1). The lasting impact of mispronouncing student names. *NEA Today.* https://www.nea.org/advocating-for-change/new-from-nea/lasting-impact-mispronouncing-students-names

McGroarty, M. (1993). Cooperative learning and second language acquisition. In D. D. Holt (Ed.), *Cooperative learning: A response to linguistic and cultural diversity* (pp. 19–46). Delta Systems and Center for Applied Linguistics.

Michaels, S., O'Connor, M. C., & Hall, M. W. (with Resnick, L. B.). (2010). *Accountable talk: Classroom conversation that works* (Version 3.1). University of Pittsburgh.

Mitchell, C. (2020, December 28). Millions of ELL students face prospect of in-person, federal testing during COVID-19. *Education Week.* https://www.edweek.org/teaching-learning/millions-of-ell-students-face-prospect-of-in-person-federal-testing-during-covid-19/2020/12

Moll, L. C. (1992). Bilingual classroom studies and community analysis: Some recent trends. *Educational Researcher, 21*(2), 20–24. https://www.jstor.org/stable/1176576

Moll, L. C., Amanti, C., Neff, D., & Gonzalez, N. (1992). Funds of knowledge for teaching: Using a qualitative approach to connect homes and classrooms. *Theory Into Practice, 21*, 132–141. https://doi.org/10.1080/00405849209543534

Moll, L. C., & Greenberg, J. (1990). Creating zones of possibilities: Combining social contexts for instruction. In L. C. Moll (Ed.), *Vygotsky and education* (pp. 319–348). Cambridge University Press.

Morcom, V. (2015). Scaffolding social and emotional learning within 'shared affective spaces' to reduce bullying: A sociocultural perspective. *Learning, Culture and Social Interaction, 6*, 77-86. https://www.sciencedirect.com/science/article/abs/pii/S2210656115000197?via%3Dihub

Moss, C. M., & Brookhart, S. M. (2012). *Learning targets: Helping students aim for understanding in today's lesson.* ASCD.

National Council of Teachers of English. (1996). *Resolution on viewing and visually representing as forms of literacy.* https://ncte.org/statement/visualformofliteracy/print/

National Institute of Child Health and Human Development (NICHHD). (2000).

Report of the National Reading Panel. Teaching children to read: An evidence-based assessment of the scientific research literature on reading and its implications for reading instruction: Reports of the subgroups (NIH Publication No. 00-4754). U.S. Government Printing Office.

National Parents Union Topline. (2020). *Coronavirus impact study.* Echelon Insights. https://nationalparentsunion.org/wp-content/uploads/2020/07/NPU-Week-8-Topline.pdf

National Research Council. (2012). *A framework for K–12 science education: Practices, crosscutting concepts, and core ideas.* Committee on a Conceptual Framework for New K–12 Science Education Standards. Board on Science Education, Division of Behavioral and Social Sciences and Education. The National Academies Press. http://www.nap.edu/read/13165/chapter/7#61

New York State Education Department. (2019). *Culturally responsive-sustaining education framework.* http://www.nysed.gov/common/nysed/files/programs/crs/culturally-responsive-sustaining-education-framework.pdf

New London Group. (1996). A pedagogy of multiliteracies: Designing social futures. *Harvard Educational Review, 66*(1), 60-93. https://doi.org/10.17763/haer.66.1.17370n67v22j160u

November, A. C. (2012). *Who owns the learning? Preparing students for success in the digital age.* Solution Tree.

OECD. (2018). *The resilience of students with an immigrant background: Factors that shape well-being.* http://dx.doi.org/10.1787/9789264292093-en

Office of Educational Technology. (n.d.). *Assessment: Measure what matters.* http://tech.ed.gov/netp/assessment-measure-what-matters

Osterman, K. (2000). Students' need for belongingness in the school community. *Review of Educational Research, 70*(3), 323–367. https://doi.org/10.3102/00346543070003323

Parker, W. C. (2006). Public discourses in schools: Purposes, problems, possibilities. *Educational Researcher, 35*(8), 11–18. https://doi.org/10.3102/0013189X035008011

Parris, H., & Estrada, L. (2019) Digital age teaching for English learners. In L. C. De Oliveira (Ed.). *The handbook of TESOL in K-12* (pp. 149-162). Wiley-Blackwell.

Partnership for 21st Century Learning (2019). *Framework for 21st Century Learning.* https://www.battelleforkids.org/networks/p21/frameworks-resources

Pearson, P. D., & Gallagher, G. (1983). The gradual release of responsibility model of instruction. *Contemporary Education Psychology, 8,* 112–123.

Pijanowski, L. (2018, March 23). *8 principles of deeper learning.* https://www.edutopia.org/article/8-principles-deeper-learning

Prensky, M. (2010). *Teaching digital natives: Partnering for real learning.* Corwin.

Pritchard, R., & O'Hara, S. (2016). Framing the teaching of academic language to English learners: A Delphi study of expert consensus. *TESOL Quarterly, 51*(2), 418 – 428. https://doi.org/10.1002/tesq.337

Purcell, K., Buchanan, J., & Friedrich, L. (2013, July 16). *The impact of digital tools on student writing and how writing is taught in schools.* http://pewinternet.org/Reports/2013/Teachers-technology-and-writing

Ritchhart, R. (2015). *Creating cultures of thinking: The 8 forces we must master to truly transform our schools.* John Wiley & Sons.

Roskos, K. A., Tabors, P. O., & Lenhart, L. A. (2009). *Oral language and early literacy in preschool: Talking, reading, and writing.* International Reading Association.

Rotella, C. (2013, September 15). *No child left untableted.* https://www.nytimes.com/2013/09/15/magazine/no-child-left-untableted.html

Sandberg, K. L., & Reschly, A. L. (2011). English learners: Challenges in assessment and the promise of curriculum-based measurement. *Remedial and Special Education, 32,* 144–154. https://doi.org/10.1177/0741932510361260

Sang, Y. (2017). Expanded territories of "literacy:" New literacies and multiliteracies. *Journal of Education and Practice, 8*(8),16-19. ISSN 2222-288X (Online)

Schleppegrell, M. J. (2012). Academic language in teaching and learning: Introduction to the special issue. *The Elementary School Journal, 112*(3), 409–418. https://www.journals.uchicago.edu/doi/10.1086/663297

Slavin, R. E. (1995). *Cooperative learning: Theory, research, and practice* (2nd ed.). Allyn & Bacon.

Snider, L. (2018). *Teaching digital resilience.* https://blog.tcea.org/digital-resilience/

Staehr Fenner, D. (2016). Fair and square assessments for ELLs. *Educational Leadership, 73*(5). http://www.ascd.org/publications/educational-leadership/feb16/vol73/num05/Fair-And-Square-Assessments-for-ELLs.aspx

Staehr Fenner, D. S., Snyder, S. (2017). *Unlocking English learners' potential: Strategies for making content accessible.* Corwin.

Stanford University. (2013). *Key principles for ELL instruction.* http://ell.stanford.edu/sites/default/files/Key%20Principles%20for%20ELL%20Instruction%20with%20references_0.pdf

Star, J. P. (2021, January 25). *Pandemic offers opportunity to reduce standardized testing.* Phi Delta Kappan. https://kappanonline.org/pandemic-offers-opportunity-to-reduce-standardized-testing/

Stevens, V. (2006, September). Revisiting multiliteracies in collaborative learning environments: Impact on teacher professional development. *TESL-EJ, 10*(2). https://www.tesl-ej.org/wordpress/issues/volume10/ej38/ej38int/

Steelcase Education Solutions. (2014). *Active learning spaces: Insights, applications & solutions* (Vol 3). www.steelcase.com/educationsolutions

Sulla, N., Bosco, T., & Marks, J. (2019). *Students taking charge implementation guide for leaders: Inside the learner-active, technology-infused classroom.* Routledge.

Takanishi, R., & Menestral, S. L. (Eds.) (2017). *Promoting the educational success of children and youth learning English: Promising futures.* National Academies Press. https://doi.org/10.17226/24677

Tharp, R. G., & Gallimore, R. (1991) *The instructional conversation: Teaching and learning in social activity* (Research Report 2). National Center for Research on Diversity and Second Language Learning, University of California. http://scholarship.org/us/item/5th0939d

Toth, M. D., & Sousa, D. A. (2019). *The power of student teams: Achieving social emotional and cognitive learning in every classroom through academic teaming.* Learning Sciences International.

Totten, S., Sills, T., Digby, A., & Russ, P. (1991). *Cooperative learning: A guide to research.* Garland.

Tucker, C. (2012). *Blended learning in grades 4–12.* Corwin.

Tucker, C. (2020). *Balance with blended learning: Partner with your students to reimagine learning and reclaim your life.* Corwin.

Tung, R., Uriarte, M., Diez, V., Gagnon, L., Stazesky, P., de los Reyes, E., et al. (2011). *Learning from consistently high performing and improving schools for English language learners in Boston Public Schools.* Center for Collaborative Education. http://files.eric.ed.gov/fulltext/ED540998.pdf

Tyrell, J. (2011, October 18). Students pen middle school survival guide. *Newsday.* http://www.newsday.com/long-island/suffolk/students- pen-middle-school-survival-guide-1.3254803

U.S. Department of Education Office of Planning, Evaluation and Policy Development (2019, May). *Supporting English learners through technology: What districts and teachers say about digital learning resources for English learners.* Volume I. https://www2.ed.gov/rschstat/eval/title-iii/180414.pdf

Victoria State Government. (2018). *Literacy teaching toolkit: Multimodal literacy.* https://www.education.vic.gov.au/school/teachers/teachingresources/discipline/english/literacy/readingviewing/Pages/litfocusmultimodal.aspx

Villegas, L., & Pompa, D. (2020). *The patchy landscape of State English Learner Policies under ESSA.* https://www.migrationpolicy

.org/research/state-english-learner
-policies-essa

Vygotsky, L. S. (1978). *Mind in society: The development of higher psychological processes.* Harvard University Press.

Whitby, T. (2014). *The relevant educator: How connectedness empowers learning.* Corwin.

WIDA. (2014). *Academic language and literacy.* https://www.wida.us/research/agenda/AcademicLanguage/index.aspx

WIDA. (2014, October). *Focus on technology in the classroom: Learning technologies and playful ecologies.* https://wida.wisc.edu/sites/default/files/resource/Focus-On-Technology-in-the-Classroom.pdf

WIDA. (2020). *WIDA English language development standards framework 2020 edition K-12.* https://wida.wisc.edu/sites/default/files/resource/WIDA-ELD-Standards-Framework-2020.pdf

Wiggins, G. P., & McTighe, J. (2005). *Understanding by design* (2nd ed.). Pearson.

Wiggins, G. P. (2012, August 27). *Less teaching and more feedback.* https://inservice.ascd.org/less-teaching-and-more-feedback/

Wilder, P. (2010). *Teaching with multiple modalities: A strategy guide.* http://www.readwritethink.org/professional-development/strategy-guides/teaching-with-multiple-modalities-30101.html

Willner, L., Rivera, C., & Acosta, B. D. (2009). Ensuring accommodations used in content assessments are responsive to English-language learners. *The Reading Teacher, 62*(8), 696–698. https://www.jstor.org/stable/20486625

Willingham, D. T. (2017). *The reading mind: A cognitive approach to understanding how the mind reads.* Jossey-Bass.

Wolpert-Gawron, H. (2017). *Just ask us: Kids speak out on student engagement.* Corwin.

Wolsey, T. D., Lapp, D., & Fisher, D. (2010). Breaking the mold in secondary schools: Creating a culture of literacy. In A. Honigsfeld & A. Cohan (Eds.), *Breaking the mold of school instruction and organization* (pp. 9–16). Rowman & Littlefield.

Wright, S. (2012). *Flipping Bloom's taxonomy.* https://shelleywright.wordpress.com/2012/05/29/flipping-blooms-taxonomy.

Zwiers, J. (2004–2005). The third language of academic English: Five key mental habits help English language learners acquire the language of school. *Educational Leadership, 62*(4), 60–63.

Zwiers, J. (2008). *Building academic language: Essential practices for content classrooms, grades 5–12.* San Francisco: Jossey-Bass.

Zwiers, J., & Crawford, M. (2009). How to start academic conversations. *Educational Leadership, 66*(7), 70–73. https://www.ascd.org/el/articles/how-to-start-academic-conversations

Index

A SAGE Publishing Company

Helping educators make the greatest impact

CORWIN HAS ONE MISSION: to enhance education through intentional professional learning.

We build long-term relationships with our authors, educators, clients, and associations who partner with us to develop and continuously improve the best evidence-based practices that establish and support lifelong learning.

Build your Visible Learning® library!

VISIBLE LEARNING

VISIBLE LEARNING FOR TEACHERS

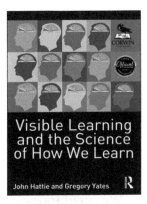

VISIBLE LEARNING AND THE SCIENCE OF HOW WE LEARN

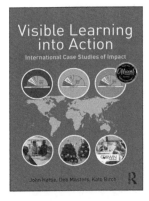

VISIBLE LEARNING INTO ACTION

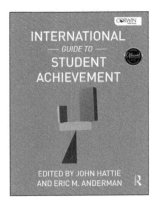

INTERNATIONAL GUIDE TO STUDENT ACHIEVEMENT

Visit corwin.com/vlbooks

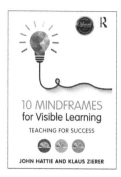

10 MINDFRAMES FOR VISIBLE LEARNING

10 MINDFRAMES FOR LEADERS

VISIBLE LEARNING FEEDBACK

DEVELOPING ASSESSMENT-CAPABLE VISIBLE LEARNERS, Grades K–12

VISIBLE LEARNING FOR LITERACY, Grades K–12

TEACHING LITERACY IN THE VISIBLE LEARNING CLASSROOM, Grades K–5, 6–12

VISIBLE LEARNING FOR MATHEMATICS, Grades K–12

TEACHING MATHEMATICS IN THE VISIBLE LEARNING CLASSROOM, Grades K–2, 3–5, 6–8, & High School

VISIBLE LEARNING FOR SCIENCE, Grades K–12

VISIBLE LEARNING FOR SOCIAL STUDIES, Grades K–12